Adventures in
Experience Design

Activities for Beginners

BY CAROLYN CHANDLER AND ANNA VAN SLEE

ILLUSTRATIONS BY SEAN K. DOVE

Adventures in Experience Design
Activities for Beginners

Carolyn Chandler and Anna van Slee

New Riders
www.newriders.com

To report errors, please send a note to errata@peachpit.com

New Riders is an imprint of Peachpit, a division of Pearson Education.

Copyright © 2014 by Carolyn Chandler and Anna van Slee

Project Editor: **Michael J. Nolan**
Development Editor: **Bob Lindstrom**
Production Editor: **Katerina Malone**
Indexer: Valerie **Haynes Perry**
Proofreader: **Rose Weisburd**
Cover and Interior Designer: **Sean K. Dove**

ISBN 13: 978-0-321-93404-8
ISBN 10: 0-321-93404-0

9 8 7 6 5 4 3 2 1

Printed and bound in the United States of America

Acclaim for Adventures

What a fun ride! *Adventures in Experience Design* cruises through the essentials, never slowing down for a lengthy explanation. Instead, you get memorable challenges, friendly, instructional feedback, and examples we can all relate to… or laugh at! Seriously, what other design book talks of "fat vs skinny questions" or narwhal enthusiasts?! Hands down the most playful, jargon-free way to jump into the vibrant world of user experience design.

> - **Stephen Anderson, author of** *Seductive Interaction Design* **and** *Mental Notes*

Identifying needs and solving them creatively will make you an invaluable designer. *Adventures in Experience Design* is an accessible and fun way to learn these powerful skills and apply them. The lessons in this book will advance your abilities as a designer and help you stand out like a pro.

> - **Jason Eastman, Strategic Partner Development, Hasbro**

Useful, practical, accessible and fun!

> - **Dave Gray, author of** *Gamestorming* **and** *The Connected Company*

Whether you are a dabbler or diver, a student or a teacher, a learner earning a degree or a DIY-er, there are plenty of ideas to pursue and exercises to attempt. I'm an educator, and when I read I cannot help but think of how to turn ideas into curriculum - which questions to pose, which activities to catalyze, which collaborations to encourage - and Carolyn and Anna have already done that. I feel as if I'm cheating on a test because the work has already been completed, and yet I'll still earn credit for offering my students an inspiring, purpose-driven, and relevant course!

> - **Eric Davis, Founder/Director of the Global Citizenship Experience & GCE High School**

Anna and Carolyn have done a brilliant job of breaking down the design processes in a fun and interactive way. A thoroughly enjoyable and inspiring read!

> - **Betsy Fore, CEO & Founder of www.Wondermento.com**

Acknowledgements

We would like to thank the education and design visionaries who were our support or inspiration (often both): Jim Jacoby, Jason Ulaszek, Eric Davis, Indi Young, Dave Gray, and Stephen Anderson.

The folks who tested our concepts, activities, and games, giving us feedback to make them even "funner": Meredith Payne, Brian Winters, Zak Orner, Patrick Thornbury, Amy Gurka, Rebecca Scherer, Megan Sanders, Kilton Hopkins, and Laura Johnson.

The people at The Starter League who provided energy, and their faces for activities and personas: Neal Sales-Griffin, Mike McGee, Veronika Goldberg, Caity Moran, Vince Cabansag, Arvin Dang, Jeff Cohen, Kelsey Mok, Josh Fabian, and Chris McKay. The savvy team at New Riders, including Bob Lindstrom, our Development Editor, Michael Nolan, our instigator, and the rest of the amazing crew: Rose Weisburd, Katerina Malone, Mimi Heft, and Valerie Haynes-Perry.

This book would not have been possible without the creative genius of Sean K. Dove. His whimsical illustrations and patiently crafted visual designs breathed life into our words.

Personal note from Carolyn:

A heart-warmed thank you to Anna, Rhett, my family, and my dear friends. You gave me the courage and heart to continue with an effort that took much of both to complete.

Personal note from Anna:

A million twinkling kisses to my Patrick for his infinite support. A huge bowl of cherry dumpling gratitude for my mom and dad for their wise advice. And a perpetual windmill of high fives with Carolyn - my professor, muse, and partner in crime.

Contents

Introduction
by Carolyn Chandler

"Too much talking, not enough doing." That was the feedback that woke me up. It was my third quarter giving a class in User Experience Design at The Starter League in Chicago, and I realized that my lecture-heavy lessons were weighing down the beginners in the class.

Design is notoriously hard to teach in shorter blocks of time. So much of design happens in the mind, where nobody can see it. It's not just about skills and sketches, but about gaining a deep and empathetic understanding of others, about taking in the context of problems, about knowing when to fight for an idea, and when to give it up. How do you explain *that*?

I began to tinker with running activities meant to create those connections in the brain, and came to realize something important.

One activity is worth a thousand words of lecture.

An activity on its own can feel like work – not that work is bad. Good work is one of the most fulfilling parts of our lives. But studies have shown that people tend to be more creative when relaxed, after laughing. And of course, a key part of design is thinking creatively. I needed to include activities that were FUN!

The missing piece fell into place when Jim Jacoby, co-founder of ADMCi (American Design and Master-Craft Initiative), connected me with Anna van Slee. Anna has an amazing understanding of the power of play. She's developed toys and games with companies such as Hasbro, and directs the playCHIC fashion show. For this book, Anna designed the games that take these design lessons home! Her creativity makes this book fresh, even for seasoned pros.

Before you dive into the book, here are some of the questions you may be asking yourself...

What's with the funny chapter names?
Experienced readers may notice a similarity between some of our process–Sponge, Spark, Splatter, Sculpt, and Storytell, and the software development life cycle–Discover, Define, Design, Develop, Deploy.

We wanted to focus on the first three steps, which are essential to Experience Design. We also wanted to bring out the playfulness of design with artistic, multi-sensory words that enhance the meaning of each stage. And we wanted the journey through the design process to sound as fun and challenging to beginners as it is for professionals.

Who is this written for?

We wrote this for anyone who is exploring Experience Design, whether they are high school or college students, book club members looking for group games, or individuals who enjoy their learning accompanied by a family-sized portion of play. Seasoned professionals may also enjoy playing these games with other team members.

If I complete this, does that mean I can say I'm a professional designer?

These adventures are meant to get your feet wet, to get you thinking like a designer, and to help you see ways that design can solve problems or address needs. There's a lot more to Experience Design than these pages can hold. We hope this book will launch your learning or help you determine if you want to pursue Experience Design as a career. If that's your passion, we think you should! (We're a bit biased.)

Can I skip around?

The book is designed to guide you through a typical design process from beginning to end. Chapters provide "building block" concepts that are brought together with a final challenge at the end of each chapter. If you're a real beginner, we recommend you go through the lessons in sequence; but those with some experience may get more out of the book by jumping to the activities that they want to practice.

Do I need a bunch of people to go through this with me?

There's plenty here for an individual to learn! However, Experience Designers work with people, and some of the games require other players to join in for the lesson to make its point. If you're reading this alone, don't be shy about inviting friends, family, co-workers, or book club members to join you in a game.

For those using this book to run activities in groups or in the classroom, we've provided The Facilitator's Guide, which is available on the book's website at:

http://adventuresxd.com

You'll also find extra design challenges there, so you can continue sharpening the skills you'll develop.

Now get ready. Open your mind. Sharpen your pencils.

And most of all, have fun!

Carolyn and Anna

Fail Forward!

It's the mantra and the rallying cry of the designer.

Failure means you tried a solution, and it didn't work.

But knowing that solution didn't work is an advantage.

It's wisdom. It's insight. It's experience you can build upon.

Fail Fearlessly!

It takes a lot of courage to try, and to fail.

But you'll never reach a brilliant solution unless you try,

and fail, and try and fail, and try and fail...

And keep trying and failing, until you get it just right.

Fail for FUN!

Be silly! Be dramatic! Be stoic! Be secretive!

Enjoy exploring unlikely answers and misfit possibilities.

They just might take you down an unexpected path to the perfect solution.

In the Adventures of Experience Design, there are no dead ends.

Starting the Adventure

A Definition:

Experience design (XD) is the practice of designing products, processes, services, events, and environments with a focus placed on the quality of the user experience and culturally relevant solutions.

The New Everyday View on Ambient Intelligence
by Marzano and Aarts
(Uitgeverij 010 Publishers, 2003)

What Is Experience Design?

Experience Design is a term most often used by those who are creating a product, such as a mobile app. It's true that most of the jobs classified as "User Experience Design" or "User Experience Research" fall in the technology field, and this book often uses digital examples for that reason. But the Experience Design perspective is much broader than a single product. It involves an immersion into the lives of the people you're designing for, and building your empathy for and understanding of them. It involves a focus on what those people are trying to do, what they'll enjoy, and their day-to-day context. A single product, like the cake at a wedding, is only one element of a person's experience.

A chef plans the menu for an upcoming wedding. He talks to the bride and groom about their family, food preferences, and location. He finds out that most of the family is Italian, and he decides to plan a menu that includes different approaches to classic Italian dishes. There will be about ten vegetarians in attendance, so one dinner option will be eggplant lasagna. The bride has a gluten allergy, so the cake will need to be gluten-free.

Across town, the florist for the wedding is designing the centerpieces for the tables. The event space has high ceilings, so she wants something tall to complement. But, she also wants guests to be able to talk to each other without having flowers in the way. She chooses a tall, thin vase with an explosion of flowers above it.

At home, the bride and groom are trying to figure out how to best move the guests from the wedding location to the cocktail area, and finally to the main reception hall. Who should help direct people? What kind of timing is necessary? Aunt Jane is in a wheelchair. Will there be an elevator or ramp for her in each location? They're also looking at table seating for dinner. How can they seat people in a way that makes everyone feel included?

All of the people described here are applying elements of Experience Design. The chef is designing a culinary experience, considering the preferences and needs of those eating. The florist is designing a product that is both pleasing and well-fitted to the environment of the reception hall. The bride and groom are designing a process to move their guests from one area to another in a way that's clear and natural.

If you've planned a party, and made decisions that you thought would enhance the experience of your guests, you've done some of this already, too! In this book, you'll learn about the techniques that professional designers use when creating a great experience for others. Maybe you'll use them to create a new process or digital app.

But first, let's find out a little more about YOU.

Why are you here?

Maybe you're here to get your feet wet, trying design techniques to figure out if you want to dive deeper into a career as an Experience Designer.

Maybe you have a particular project or product in mind, and want to take it through some of the steps that designers use to envision and refine solution ideas creatively and collaboratively.

Maybe you just like your learning with a large helping of play!

Whatever the reason, you'll be glad you're here. There's power in understanding the needs of others, and creating something that really engages or empowers them. And what's fantastic is you don't have to consider yourself a professional designer to solve problems using Experience Design.

Going through the building blocks, challenges, and activities in this book will give you a designer's-eye view of the world. You'll try your hand at different techniques for gaining empathy for others, come up with great solution ideas, brainstorm multiple concepts, refine the best of them, and spread the word about your creation.

So you want to travel the path of design? There are riches and dangers ahead. Your feet are on the trail now. Stretch out and get ready with a warm-up activity that will open your mind and set your sights!

About THIS Experience

This is an activity-driven book that will take you through the kind of process professional designers use to create memorable experiences.

Each chapter introduces a stage in the design process. You'll find concise descriptions of key concepts for that stage, along with activities to practice important related skills.

Play the games to make the lessons come to life in a fun, often social way!

Concepts explored throughout each chapter are brought together in a final challenge, in which you work on a design solution of your own.

The Path Ahead

Here's the treasure map that will guide your way...

You are here

SPONGE!

What activity do you want to improve? For whom? What problems do they face now? Try these techniques to gain insights about the people you're designing for.

You'll Explore:
- Working with assumptions
- Asking research questions
- Basic body language
- Research in the field

SPARK!

Use insights to define your audience and the problems they face. Generate Solution Ideas by trying Spark questions that challenge and inspire.

You'll Explore:
- Finding a problem's root cause
- Quantitative vs. qualitative data
- Different solution types
- Questions that help you generate ideas
- Defining your idea

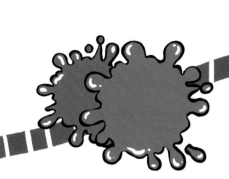

SPLATTER!

Visualize a concept for your solution ideas. Brainstorm multiple concepts with others to generate many in a short time frame! Find new ideas in the wonderful mess you made.

You'll Explore:

- Sketching concepts
- Working with constraints
- Brainstorming many concepts
- Finding patterns

SCULPT!

Cut out unnecessary concepts and features. Refine your creation visually. Test it out!

You'll Explore:

- Creating design principles
- Understanding the context of use
- Planning features that delight
- Prioritizing features
- Testing your idea with others

STORYTELL!

Express the importance and meaning of your solution.

You'll Explore:

- The power of brands
- Expressing a brand's voice
- Marketing your solution
- Speaking to your audience

Warm-Up Game
Photo Safari

Goal

Become aware of all the good and bad designs that you encounter throughout your typical day.

What You'll Need
- A camera
- Photoshop
  - *OR* a social network that lets you share pictures, such as Facebook, Instagram, Pinterest, or Tumblr.

Step 1: Picture Day

Starting the first thing in the morning, use your camera to take pictures of good designs and bad designs - things that make your life easier, or harder. Remember, design can be digital as well as physical, so screen captures count, too! Keep snapping photos all day long, right up until bed time. Ideally, you want to capture at least 30 total photos.

Step 2: Sort

Review your shots, and separate the examples of good design from the bad, keeping them in chronological order. Once you finish sorting, you will have two folders of images: one with all the good designs you encountered throughout the day, and one with all the bad designs.

Step 3: Channel Your Inner Ken Burns
- *Photoshop*: Import all your photos into one Photoshop file, then arrange as directed below.
- *Printer & Posterboard*: Print out all your photos individually, then arrange them as directed below.

Arrange all the pics of good design in a row, so that from left to right they represent a visual timeline of your day. The row should start on the far left with the first image of good design that you took at the start of your day, and end with the last picture of good design that you captured at the end of your day. Do the same for your pictures of bad design.

- *Social*: Depending on which social network you chose, arrange your pics in two albums, photo streams, etc., and in chronological order.

Sponge!

You're About to:

Challenge your own assumptions

Develop your skills in empathy

Learn to read body language

Interview a rock star

Play the anthropologist

Did You Know?

You're probably most familiar with manufactured sponges, but those are inspired by animals that live in the sea! Although sponges seem soft, they are actually one of the toughest animals around. If they're cut up, the pieces will regenerate into new sponges.

Sponges move water in and out of channels in their bodies, filtering their food from the water. In this chapter, like a sponge, you'll soak in information and filter it for the elements that will help you generate design ideas.

If you had to pick a body part that's most closely associated with the act of designing, you may think of HANDS. After all, designers are creating all sorts of things, from websites to houses. And to create these things, designers use their hands to sketch out ideas with pen and paper, or to create models for what they plan to build.

Or, you may pick the BRAIN. You need a good, solid brain to come up with interesting ideas and to plan out the details. Without question, the brain is deeply involved throughout the whole process of design.

But before an idea of yours becomes really solid, your brain has to partner up with your EYES and EARS, to *observe* and *listen* to people. Like a sponge, you must soak in everything that surrounds you so you can understand how people think and act, and figure out what they really need. You also ought to absorb the environment around them and the tools they use from day to day. Designers call these things the "context of use" for the products they design.

In this chapter, you'll explore ways to sponge up details of the world around you so that you can form relevant design ideas. And to be really creative, you have to soak in information that's outside of your daily routine.

⚠ WARNING!

It can be hard to observe things without bias getting in the way! You're a human being,* and humans tend to make assumptions about other humans. Sometimes assumptions are correct and sometime they mislead you. That means it's important to know when you're making them, and to validate them as true or false.

*The authors have made an assumption that you're a human being, and we apologize to all other intelligent life forms including but not exclusive to: aliens, monsters, talking animals, fairies, leprechauns, winged monkeys, comic book characters, action figures, and alternate-universe versions of human beings (non-evil).

In this adventure you will **SPONGE** - immerse yourself in the lives of other people so that you can find some good, meaty problems to solve through design. You'll also gain an important context that will help you generate ideas and make good design decisions later!

Questions to Ponder:
- How do you a solve a problem that's not your own?
- How do you find out if you're making the wrong assumptions about someone or something?
- Why don't people always say exactly what's on their minds? How can you tell when they don't?

What You'll Do:
- Figure out the assumptions you have made about people. Find out if there's truth to them - or if the assumptions are wrong! If you design with the wrong assumptions, your creation may never be used.
- Learn about the people you're designing for by asking good questions (and yes, there are bad questions!).
- Develop skills in active listening and observation, to go beyond the words people say - and gather information that will give you true insights.

When You Assume...

Everyone makes assumptions, especially when they have limited experiences to draw from. For example, if you saw hominid bones at the archaeology museum in your town, you may assume that you'd find them at the same kind of museum in another city.

Assumptions can cause problems when you design something based on them, and then find out that they were wrong.

For example, you could design a mobile application for bus drivers, and then find out that they can't use it safely while driving the bus. Or you may find out that many bus drivers don't have the kind of phone you designed for!

Working with Assumptions

Assumptions are ideas you've formed about people or situations, based on your past experiences or on things you've heard from other sources.

For example, you may make the assumption that CIA officers are always running around in exotic locations, especially if you've seen them only in movies or on TV. (In reality, most CIA officers spend a lot of time behind a desk.)

When you're designing something, it's important that you identify the assumptions you're making and understand when they might be causing you to form the wrong conclusions. Don't ignore your assumptions completely, but write them down and then *validate* them - prove them true, untrue, or only sometimes true - by going into the field and conducting research. Observe the people you're designing for, and ask them well-formed questions. You'll gain a lot more real-world information that way.

If you don't get out into the field to observe people and talk to them, you will use only your assumptions as a basis for understanding the people you're designing for. Designing under those circumstances is difficult - if not impossible - to do well!

So, you'll be heading out into the field to observe people and ask them questions! Before you get started, let's find out what makes a good question good, and a bad question bad.

Game:
Field Character Study

Goal

Hone your observational skills and avoid the pitfalls of assumptions by correctly guessing what a stranger is going to order at a cafe.

What You'll Need

Whatever best enables you to quickly and easily record your observations: pen and paper, tablet, laptop, etc.

Step 1: Set Up in the Field

Go to a (preferably busy) coffee shop or cafe, and set up at a table with a clear view of the customer line, register, and order/delivery area.

Step 2: Watch & Record

Pick a person - any person! - at the end of the line. Begin recording as many observations about that person as possible. Try to jot down at least 10 observations before he (or she) gets near he front of the line.

Step 3: Make a Guess

When the person nears the front of the line, guess what he will order based on your observations. Write down your guess.

Step 4: Check Your Guess

What did the person you were observing finally order? Write down the actual order next to your guess.

Step 5: Repeat!

Go through Steps 1-4 again with at least eight different people. Try to pick people of many different ages and types.

Step 6: Analyze Your Results

Were there any similarities among the people for whom you guessed correctly? What assumptions did you make that were correct? What assumptions did you make that were incorrect? Isolate those assumptions as statements. For example, "I guessed younger people would order sweeter drinks because I assumed kids eat more sugar." When are assumptions helpful? When are they inhibiting? Were you able to guess correctly for the majority of people in your study?

Variations

Try to analyze one particular type of person. For example, observe only white, middle-aged men.

Not a coffee drinker? Try out this game at your favorite restaurant, just hang on to a menu for reference!

Game:
Maître Do, Maître Don't

Goal

Level up your investigative skills and correctly guess what your partner would order from a menu. (No cheating!!! Don't peek at the menu until after you have completed Step 2.)

What You'll Need

- Something to write with
- Stopwatch or clock

Step 1: Quiz Your Partner

Interview your partner about his or her preferences. You will use these interview results to judge what your partner would order off a menu, so try to ask questions that can help you quickly rule things in or out. For example, don't ask, "Do you like ice cream?" Instead, a better question might be: "Do you have any food allergies?" And if the answer is yes, "Which ones?"

Step 2: Your Turn to Be Interviewed

Spend five minutes answering questions from your partner. Be honest!

Step 3: Check Out the Menu

Flip to page 141 and explore the menu on your own. Don't talk about it with your partner yet. Bon Appetit!

Step 4: Place Your Order

Imagine that you have $20 to spend. What would you get? Record your order, and don't worry about tax or tip. You only get five minutes to make up your mind. Your partner should be deciding what she would order too.

Step 5: Order for Your Partner, Too

What do you think your partner would order with her $20? Write down your guess.

Step 6: Compare Orders

Who was able to guess more dishes correctly - you or your partner? That person is the winner!

However, everybody wins when you ask good questions. Probe your reasoning with the aid of your partner. Why did you pick certain items for her? On which of your interview questions did you base your assumptions? Explore the question/assumption tactics that were the most successful.

12

Creating Research Questions

You can ask many kinds of questions during an interview. Think of those questions as being either skinny or fat.

SKINNY QUESTIONS

Skinny questions can be answered in just a few words - sometimes only one! For example, if you ask, Did you floss your teeth before leaving the house today?, you'll probably get a "yes" or "no" answer. Skinny questions may also be called *closed* questions because they have a small set of common answers, and sometimes those answers can be proven true or false. If your interview subject answers "yes," but someone else was there and knows he didn't, he may be busted!

Generally, skinny questions are better for surveys or quizzes like those you take online. They allow you to compare simple answers across a large number of people, so you make statements like "Twenty percent of those surveyed answered that they did floss that morning."

Other examples of skinny questions:
What is the capital of France?
Who is your favorite actor?

FAT QUESTIONS

Fat questions can't easily be answered with one or two words. They require the subject to explain her opinion or rationale for doing something, or to explain a process she uses. If someone says she doesn't like to floss, you could ask her, "What do you dislike about flossing your teeth?" The question is more *open* because the person needs to think about flossing and identify her own reasons for disliking it. Perhaps it's because she thinks flossing takes too much time, or because her gums are sensitive and it's uncomfortable for her to floss.

Fat questions are better for interviews that you conduct in person or over the phone. They lead to more detail about a particular person's experience and give you a richer understanding of her thoughts and feelings.

Other examples of fat questions:
How do you study for a hard test?
Tell me about a time you laughed so hard that you cried.

Activity:
Rock On, _____!

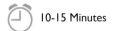

14

Write the name of your favorite rock star on the line above. Now write down some questions you'd ask him or her during an interview.

SKINNY QUESTIONS

may start with: Who were...?   When did...?
                      What is...?   Is it true that...?

When did play your first show?

_____

_____

_____

_____

_____

_____

_____

FAT QUESTIONS

may start with: Why..?   What if...?
                      How...?   Tell me about...

How does it feel to be famous?

_____

_____

_____

_____

_____

_____

_____

Activity:
Lasso the Leaders

 5-10 Minutes   1+ Player

When writing a question for research, try to avoid writing it in a way that implies a particular answer or that assumes a person already feels a certain way. These are called *leading questions* because they lead people to an answer, whether or not that answer is the honest one.

It's also good to avoid asking questions that seem to accuse people of something (which can make them feel uncomfortable) or that use extreme words such as "always" (because people rarely do the same thing all the time).

Circle the letters of questions below that are badly worded, and explain why you chose them. We started you off with one answer. When you're ready, you'll find the rest of the answers on page 142.

A. What are you typically doing before class starts?

B. Why are you always late for work?

C. Tell me why you like this painting.

D. What makes Jennifer Lawrence such a great actor?

E. What do you tend to do when you're on vacation?

F. Why don't you floss more?

Letter:	Reason:
B	it uses the extreme word "always" which is probably not true.

More Than Words

Only a small part of communication is about the actual words that are said. Think about:

- The words of the question you ask *and* the way you ask it. Is your tone casual or formal? Friendly or angry?
- The words of the person's answer, and his tone when answering
- The *body language* you're both expressing (more on that shortly!)
- Any pressures he may feel in answering a certain way (such as pressure to agree with you, or to represent himself in a positive way)
- The context around you. If small children are around, an interview subject may not feel comfortable sharing details on a horror movie that he likes!

Active Listening

Asking good questions is a very important skill when gathering information, but just as important is the ability to not just hear, but really listen to the responses you get.

Active listening is a technique that assures your interviewee that you sincerely care about what he's saying, and helps you identify areas where you may not be understanding him correctly. When you demonstrate active listening, you can build trust, avoid misunderstandings, and have more open conversations.

One great technique is to repeat a person's answer back to him to confirm it. When you do this using words that are similar (but not identical) to his, you're *paraphrasing*. Here's an example:

> You: How do you feel when you're about to go to the dentist?
>
> John: I get a bit nervous, every time I'm about to head into the room!
>
> You: So the visit with the dentist makes you nervous?
>
> John: Well, I don't mind the actual teeth cleaning, which is all that usually happens. But what if she finds a cavity or tells me I need to have a root canal? Most of the time she doesn't find anything that needs a fix, but I definitely heave a sigh of relief when I know for sure!

Body language is also a key part of active listening. If people are uncomfortable, they won't be as engaged with the questions you're asking, or as open about their responses. Let's take a closer look at what we say without using words.

Basic Body Language

You'll get better information from a person who's relaxed. How can you tell when a conversation is going well?

Facial Expression

This person's face is tight and controlled. His polite smile could mean he's uncomfortable or skeptical.

This smile is more relaxed, meaning there's a good chance he's genuinely enjoying the conversation.

Arms

Crossed arms could mean he's cold, but it could also mean he's feeling guarded or defensive.

Open arms indicate that he's comfortable. His hands are on his hips, which could mean he's feeling confident.

Body Orientation

You can see from his legs, hips, and shoulders that he's oriented away from you slightly.

A straight-on orientation indicates a more fully engaged person.

Feet

Feet tend to point where the body wants to go. He has one foot pointed to the door. That's a bad sign.

Here both feet are pointing towards you; so he's probably really listening, and not plotting an escape route.

It's in the Smile

People who are uncomfortable, or just not completely engaged in a conversation, will often smile politely - but their faces give them away. A tighter face usually represents a fake smile. A genuine smile is more relaxed, and leads to more crinkling of the eyes and a wider grin. You may also notice that a head tilt and shoulder movement goes with a real smile, like the person is giving a small laugh.

AT REST

FAKE

GENUINE

AT REST

FAKE

GENUINE

Activity:
Find the Fake

Below you'll see a variety of people with their faces at rest.

Which of the smiles in this second row are genuine, and which are fake?

☐ Fake ☐ Genuine   ☐ Fake ☐ Genuine   ☐ Fake ☐ Genuine   ☐ Fake ☐ Genuine   ☐ Fake ☐ Genuine

Make your guesses...

Answers on page 143

The Next Top Model

Once you better understand a group of people through observation and interviewing, you can create a *model* of them, which is a diagram that visually expresses your understandings. Having a user model will help you later when you're trying to design for the group, and need to remember what you'd seen and heard from them. It will also help you represent them to other people on your design or development team.

There are several kinds of user models. Here are a few of the most common:

Artsy Arthur

Arthur is an art student who specializes in sculpture. He's planning on applying to two different art schools.

PERSONAS

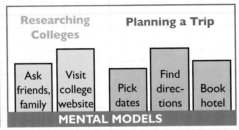

Researching Colleges   **Planning a Trip**

Ask friends, family | Visit college website | Pick dates | Find direc-tions | Book hotel

MENTAL MODELS

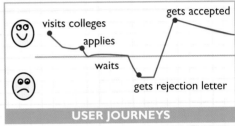

gets accepted
visits colleges
applies
waits
gets rejection letter

USER JOURNEYS

Personas are small, focused biographies of a fictional person. They're meant to represent the goals, activities, frustrations and motivations of a specific type of user.

Mental models represent user behaviors and steps related to a goal, such as "visiting potential colleges." They highlight the ways people think about the goals and the activities involved.

Journeys are sequential models representing behaviors and feelings over a longer period of time, like a journey for applying for, being accepted to, and attending a college.

Ideally, all of these models are based on research that you've completed with a larger group of potential users - for example, 12 to 30 people. The models represent key trends and common needs found during your research.

We won't be delving deeply into models in this book, but if you want to level up and try your hand at personas or other models, you can find more information at the end of this chapter in "Challenges You Can Chew."

A persona-style model is still a useful way to represent the people you're interviewing, so take a look at an example. You'll be using a similar format to capture profiles during your final challenge. Which begins... now!

Spotlight: Personas

BEGINNER BEN

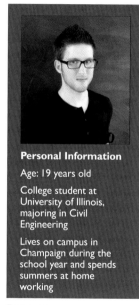

Personal Information

Age: 19 years old

College student at University of Illinois, majoring in Civil Engineering

Lives on campus in Champaign during the school year and spends summers at home working

Ben uses:

About Ben

Ben has wanted to be an engineer ever since he got his first model plane set at age 12. Now he's an outgoing, bright engineering student who gets good grades at school. He knows he currently lacks the experience to get the job he really wants after he graduates, and he wants to find ways to gain that experience now.

Goals

- Study and intern abroad in Copenhagen for a year

- Gain the experience that will help him start working immediately after completing his undergraduate degree

Frustrations

- Ben is learning hard skills in his classes, but hasn't been able to apply them to any jobs or internships directly related to his area of interest.

- Writing a resume can be difficult. He wants to highlight the skills he's taking in class, but most job sites focus on professional experience.

Activities

- By day, Ben attends class, plays flag football, and volunteers with his fraternity.

- By night, he works part-time and occasionally attends on-campus workshops about finding internships and jobs.

Personas are not real people themselves, but they pull together insights you've gotten from talking to a number of real people in the same general group.

For example, if you're trying to design a site that allows students to find internships in their areas of interest, you may create a persona like Beginner Ben.

You would interview or survey several students to find out their:

Goals: The main things they want to accomplish, related to the problem you're trying to solve

Frustrations: Aspects of the current situation that are causing them pain or annoyance

Activities: Tasks they have to accomplish, or events they have to react to

Demographics: Facts such as age, location, income, and ethnicity

When you're designing, personas help you think of the features a group will need and care about, and how to best address them.

Tips for the Field

A lot of TV interviews cover a single topic or an opinion. But to grow empathy with someone, you'll have to ask them questions about things.

Learn about the things that frustrate them, make them happy, excite them, or make them angry. Try also to get them to tell you stories so that you can learn about their motivations, values, and reasoning.

Be respectful. Tell each person how much time you need before you start. Aim for 15-30 minutes based on the number of questions you have.

Take note of environmental elements that may influence their experience, such as crowds, spaces, pathways, and noise levels.

THE SPONGE CHALLENGE!

For your final chapter challenge, choose a **Challenge statement,** and then get out in the field to sponge up information that you'll take into the next step! Your Challenge should have the form of:

"Make.... [this activity] [improved in this way] for [this user type]."

ACTIVITY	IMPROVEMENT	USER TYPE
Driving	more safe for	bus drivers
Studying	more fun for	high school students
Finding music	less expensive for	parents of small children
Pick one	here too	and who!

To come up with a lot of statements at once, try mixing and matching options from different columns. (In the current table, for example, you could decide to make "driving more fun for parents of small children.") Or get together with a couple of friends, and each of you choose a different column and list four things in that column using the cut-out cards on the next page. Read them off by number and mix and match between you to build statements that make sense (not all of them will). Pick one and discuss what that Challenge statement means to you.

Decide on a Challenge statement. Then find **three to five** people who represent the chosen type of user, and interview them to better understand their current context. Try to observe people before and after the interview as they go through that activity. You can use the following worksheets to help you get started.

Challenge Cards

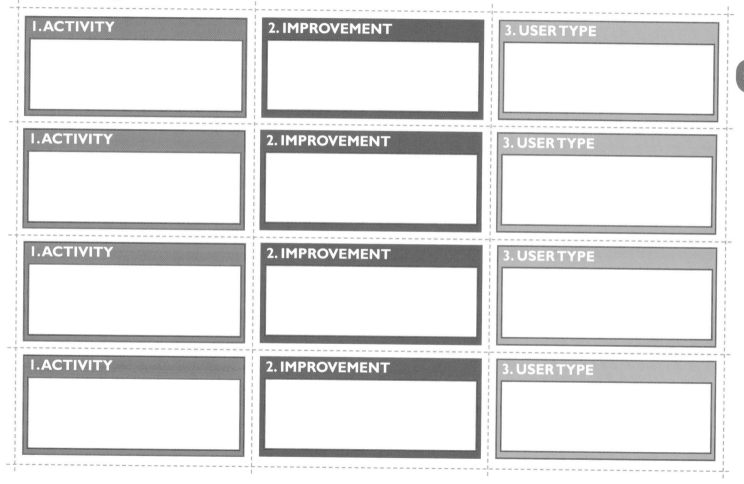

Artifacts!

When you go out in the field, like an anthropologist, you ideally collect artifacts. These can be digital (such as photos) or physical items (such as free instructional pamphlets).

You'll come across things you won't expect, but that will give you great ideas for needs you could address through design. You can also plan for some. Can you think of any photos or other artifacts you might want to collect? Make a checklist:

- ☐ _____
- ☐ _____
- ☐ _____
- ☐ _____
- ☐ _____
- ☐ _____
- ☐ _____

Make a Plan, Man

Write down the assumptions you have about the activity you've chosen.

Where do people tend to do it?

_____

What materials or tools do they need (a car, a pencil, a mobile phone)?

_____

Why is it important to improve this activity for this user group? What are the consequences now without that improvement?

_____

_____

Who are you going to interview? Where?

_____

What particular activities would you like to have them show you, or describe? (For driving, you could include getting gas, dealing with traffic, and parking.)

_____

Now, write up at least 10 questions that help people share their experiences. Interview three to five people from your user group, and use information from their answers to fill out a profile for each person. Good luck!

Profile of (Name): _____

Sketch or affix a portrait

Personal info:

Age: _____

Location: _____

_____

Other Facts:

_____

_____

_____

_____

About this Person:

_____

_____

_____

_____

Goals:

_____

_____

_____

Frustrations:

_____

_____

_____

Activities:

_____

_____

_____

26

The Debrief

Now you should have a nice, chaotic mix of notes, pictures, pamphlets and other fun artifacts that represent the information you've collected during your interviews and observations.

If you have a spare wall, or a moveable poster, you could make a collage of your artifacts and pictures. This will help you in the next chapters as you think of ideas for solutions to design.

Maybe you already have some ideas about specific problems you'd like to solve rolling around in there, too!

In the next chapter we'll talk about about digging into your insights to find ideas that address real needs, and perform some basic sketching exercises that will help you move from communicating with words to communicating visually.

Spark!

You're About to:

Ask "why, why, why" like a two-year-old child

Mix numbers and words in strange new ways

Predict the future of fashion

Play the architect for a school

Pitch an idea to the shark tank

Did You Know?

Sparks are caused by the friction of two substances, where one has a strong negative charge and the other has a strong positive charge. When you get a shock in dry weather, your hand has a strong enough positive charge to react with the negative charge on that door handle that zapped you.

In the Experience Design process, sparks come from understanding the negative aspects of the current situation (problems, and their consequences) and thinking of creative actions you can take for positive change. This kind of spark will lead to great ideas for solutions to design.

Sometimes an idea can come to you so suddenly that it's hard to pinpoint all of the elements that went into it. Some wonderful combination of things brewed in your brain until a connection was made.

When you make that new mental connection, your brain rewards you by releasing pleasure chemicals that make you feel good. Did you just come up with a great word to use in Words with Friends? "Well done!" says your brain. "Here, have some dopamine!" Ahhhhh.

Because creating new connections and ideas is so tied to pleasure, it can be easy to get attached to a particular solution. After all, that solution just FELT good so it must be the best, right? That way of thinking can be dangerous for designers, though, because that solution may not be the best one. Maybe it doesn't fix the real issue that's causing a problem. Maybe it's a relatively insignificant part of the problem, not worth the effort you put into it. How do you know?

In this chapter, you'll focus on sparking great solution ideas (the positive charge) with information about the problems and its consequences (the negative charge). When both sides of that are intense enough to cause a spark, you know you're on a good path.

In Sponge, you immersed yourself into a situation to gain valuable insights. That will ground you for this adventure—and being grounded is important when you're dealing with electricity!

So dim the lights. Gather your needs. Start brewing information in your brain. Let's find out what ignites your imagination!

In this adventure you will **SPARK** an idea for what you'd like to design by taking the knowledge that you gained when immersing (**SPONGE**) and applying your skills in problem-solving. By the end of the chapter you will identify the problems that you want to solve for a particular group of people, form questions to help you generate possible solutions, and choose one solution to design as you move on to SPLATTER.

Questions to Ponder:
- How do you figure out which problems you should try to tackle?
- What happens when you solve the wrong problem?
- How can you communicate the urgency of a problem that you want to solve?
- How do you generate ideas that will produce solutions to a problem?

What You'll Do:
- Dig beyond the surface of a problem to figure out the root needs or issues that may be causing it.
- Discover the impact of the problem you'd like to address.
- Conduct a creative brainstorm session to find solution ideas.
- Create a Spark Frame that describes your chosen solution idea, and why it's important.
- Pitch your proposal to others!

Introducing: The Spark Frame

So what is a Spark really? A Spark is a question that helps you generate solution ideas for real problems. A good Spark Frame like the one below outlines the overall challenge, the related problems you've found, your Spark, and some possible creative solution ideas. Let's break this down, using this book as an example!

CHALLENGE

Make this activity...	improved in this way (more, less...)	for these people:
learning about experience design	*more fun and accessible*	*curious beginners*
	(more on page 31)	

SPARK

Considering these problems...	we'll spark solution ideas by asking:
Design practices are best learned in a hands-on way, but not everyone can learn straight from a designer.	*How might we use playful, hands-on activities to expose people to the power of design?*
The full design process can be daunting!	
(more on page 35)	(more on page 42)

SOLUTION IDEAS

Develop a video game that requires individuals to design their way out of a sticky situation	Host a design challenge event staffed by volunteer designers	Write a book that uses activities and games to explain design practices
		(more on page 46)

Choosing Improvements

Let's dig deeper into our original challenge in order to explore elements of your Spark Frame. In Sponge, you chose a type of improvement to explore. A good Spark Frame includes improvements that are ideally measurable, so you can tell if your solution really has made an impact. Two fairly different types are quantitative and qualitative.

QUANTITATIVE IMPROVEMENTS

Quantitative improvements are based on numerical data (quantities), and are gathered by tracking and measuring the concrete results of a test. For example, an objective improvement would be to make something:

- More effective (the same amount of effort from the user has a greater impact when the activity is performed). These shoes are more effective than others because they give you a higher jump with no extra push on your part.

Other numerically-driven improvements include making something:

- More efficient, (The activity can be completed in less time, or with fewer resources.)
- More predictable. (Each time you perform the activity, you tend to get the same measurable result.)
- Safer. (Fewer accidents or injuries happen when the activity is performed.)

QUALITATIVE IMPROVEMENTS

Qualitative improvements focus on qualities, such as users' perceptions of an activity or how they feel during it. They are more word-oriented, and often more inspirational. For example, you could make an activity:

- More luxurious
- More fun
- Less stressful
- More glamorous

These improvements are harder to measure, but there are ways. For example, you could give two surveys to your user group to find out how they felt about the activity before and after using your new design.

You may want to have both a qualitative and quantitative improvement in mind to be sure you're making an impact - and delighting your users, too. Biking can be safer AND more luxurious for the bald!

Activity:
Measure Up: The Object of Your Affection

 20 Minutes   1+ Player

Ah, Valentine's Day. It's a holiday with a lot of commercial appeal. Imagine that you've been hired by the city to make the holiday healthier and more affordable for its citizens. You've already made a series of pretty specific recommendations to improve citizens' health and budgets on Valentine's Day, but now you need to let the city know how you plan to measure the impact of your solutions. How will you gauge whether or not your solutions will be successful? Read the statements below, and then write in your objective measurement after each one.

How would you measure your results if you were trying to make Valentine's Day treats healthier for children?

I'd measure the number of cavities that kids got in the months after the holiday, compared with the number of cavities last year at the same time

How would you measure your results if you were trying to make valentines cards easier to share for students?

How would you measure your results if you were trying to make mail-order flowers less expensive for women?

How would you measure your results if you were trying to make chocolates less fattening for men?

Game:
WORD Herd

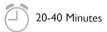 
Goal
Learn about subjective measurement first hand by assessing a tattoo sleeve as an individual and as a group.

Helpful Hint: The bigger the group, the better the results

What You'll Need
- Something to write on that everyone can see: A chalkboard, white board, or piece of poster board

Step 1: Sleeve It to Me
Check out the tattoo design on the following page. How does the design make you feel? Would you get this tattoo?

Step 2: Evaluate the Tattoo
Now look at the list of words to the right of the design. Circle the words that you feel describe that tattoo sleeve design. For example, if you think the tattoo is funny, then circle the word "funny." Circle as many words as you want.

Step 3: Plot out the Cloud
Designate someone to be the Word Herd recorder to stand by the board or poster and record the group's reactions. Pick someone to start with and have that person read out all the words that he circled. The recorder will write down each word on the board for all to see, leaving plenty of space (around 12 inches) between words. When the recorder has written down all the words that the first person circled, move on to another person in the group and have her do the same.

If the second person circled the same word as the first person, the recorder does not need to write that word down again, he only has to put a circle around the word he has already written. But make sure to write down any words that the second person chose, which the first person did not.

Continue to go around the group, until everyone has has a chance to read their words. Every time someone chooses a word that was already been written down, add another circle around it. Eventually, the most popular words will have many circles around them.

Game:
WORD Herd con't.

Step 4: Ya Herd?

What were the results of your Word Herd? Did everyone tend to agree on a few words, or were the results all over the map? Did more popular words tend to relate to each other, or were they opposites? Why do you think some people picked the same words, while other people picked different ones? If you were the tattoo artist, how might you change the design to appeal to more people in your group?

Step 5: Play It Again, Sam

What else can you assess with a Word Herd? Just about anything! Try reviewing a corporate logo with a group. Or, put the visual branding of any of your solutions from this book's activities to the test.

- Funny
- Cool
- Out of Style
- Impractical
- Painful
- Controversial
- Pointless
- Feasible
- Masculine
- Feminine
- Foolish
- Classic
- Dirty
- Weird
- Enviable
- Beautiful
- Ugly
- Attractive
- Artistic
- Modern
- Unprofessional
- Expensive
- Clever
- Hip
- Trendy

Defining the Problem

Henry Ford, inventor of the automobile, is famous for saying, "If I had asked people what they wanted, they would have said faster horses."

In other words, people had a need to get from Point A to Point B more quickly, but horses were what they had. Most would have had a hard time imagining something could replace horses completely. People usually describe their behaviors or suggest improvements based on their current understandings and frustrations.

Getting to the root cause of a problem is an excellent way to think bigger when designing. You can do this by asking Why (during an interview, or to yourself) multiple times until you feel that you've gotten to the source of a series of problems.

Let's say you're trying to decrease the number of morning tardies in a high school. In the example to the right, you could have stopped at the first suggestion that the student made to propose a solution (marked with a star *). Or you could keep going and uncover an entirely different set of problems.

Try it yourself! Ask a friend about a recent time when he or she ran late for class, work, or an appointment.

Example:

You: I'm trying to understand different reasons that students end up coming in late to class. Could you tell me about a recent time?

Student: Last Tuesday I was about five minutes late to my first class.

You: Why did you end up running late that day?

Student: I had to walk through the whole school that day. I wish I had a moving walkway or something to make it faster.*

You: Why did you have to walk through the whole school?

Student: My mom dropped me off at the farthest door that time.

You: Why wasn't she able to drop you off at the closer door?

Student: She was running late, too, and the close door is hard to get to.

You: Why is it so hard to get to?

Student: Everyone drops people off there. The car line gets really backed up, and once you're in line you can't easily get out.

You: Why does the line get so backed up?

Student: There's just a small "dropoff" area for that door and it's right by the track. And sometimes the track team is walking back to the gym from early practice, so the cars have to stop for the people.

What problems can you see within this exchange? Which do you think would be the best to solve? Often, you'll want to create a solution that has a great impact. But how can you anticipate solutions that will?

GYM

MAIN HALL

CLASSROOM CLASSROOM

DROPOFF LINE

FIRE LANE (MUST REMAIN OPEN WHEN UNSUPERVISED)

TO TRACK →

Let's say you observe the "dropoff" area mentioned on page 35. If you sketch it, or ask drivers to tell you how they feel about the process, that's qualitative data.

If you count the number of cars that join the line during a specific half-hour period, or the average time it takes for one car to make it through, that's quantitative.

Cracked Case Study: The Yolk's on You

In the fall of 1969, 100 college freshman architecture students - eager to start solving problems - gathered for their first design class at the University of Illinois at Chicago. Among them was Frank Gorski.

The class had three professors, Frank recalls, and they started class with an anecdote. Have you ever opened a carton of eggs at the grocery store and found a broken egg inside? The class muttered consent. The professors went on to assign the students their very first design problem: Every year, millions of eggs are broken in transit. Design a better container to prevent eggs from breaking.

Frank and his classmates came up with some really cool solutions. One guy created a carton that mimicked an egg, itself, in which one egg was suspended with rubber bands in an egg-shaped package. "Not very practical [because it only held one egg]," says Frank. "But it worked really, really well. They threw it down stairs, out of a car window - it never broke." Frank himself designed a carton that used springs and triangles to distribute the force on the egg and leveraged the egg's vertical strength. Other students wrapped eggs in foam and wire. One student put eggs in dense foam-rubber

softballs. Weeks and weeks were dedicated to creating these solutions. The final exam consisted of students dropping their egg cartons off the roof of the college to see if the eggs would break or not.

During the final class for that project, however, the professors revealed that, in relation to the number of eggs that are shipped nationwide every year, very few are actually broken in transit. The students had assumed that the professor's word, backed up by a personal anecdote that they could relate to, constituted a real problem. It did not. They'd spent weeks solving a problem that didn't exist!

Today, Frank is a licensed architect and Chief Plan Examiner for the Cook County Department of Building and Zoning in Illinois. He still uses the lesson he learned in that class every day.

"Make sure you are solving a problem that's really a problem," Frank says. "Question all your assumptions. When you go to solve a problem, you can't preconceive what that outcome's going to be. Do research and find good data that supports your problem, and illustrates a real need."

Understanding Impact

You can figure out some of the impact of an existing situation by gathering data about the results that it produces. Situations that have a lot of negative results and little to no positive results are often good to focus on when looking for new, high-impact design ideas. Let's look deeper into quantitative and qualitative data.

QUANTITATIVE DATA

As we mentioned earlier when discussing improvements, results that are quantitative focus on numbers and can be measured, counted, or precisely defined. The findings are often expressed with tables of numbers, or more visually, with graphs or infographics.

You can gather quantitative data by measuring or counting things yourself, or by using data tracked digitally (such as online tools that track how many people have viewed a particular website).

If you don't have the ability to measure something yourself, see if you can find good secondary resources for the information, such as studies completed by relatively objective research organizations. (See the sidebar on page 52.) Good outside resources can show you trends among a larger group of people, or the impact of a certain situation over time.

QUALITATIVE DATA

If you completed the interview challenge in Sponge, you've already gathered some qualitative data! You can gather it through observation and interviews; and your findings can be expressed using sketches, photos, or quotes that describe people's feelings, behaviors, and motivations.

Interviewing people is not the only useful way to gather this data. In fact, if you only talk to people, you may not come up with some of the most distinctive and amazing design ideas!

Watching people performing an activity will give you great first-hand information about what they're struggling with. You can ask them to show you, or even better, watch them in a public space (or any place where you're invited) as they try to do something. You'll also gather inportant information about the environment around them.

Game:
Fashion a Plan

Goal

Learn the difference between quantitative and qualitative research. Try to predict what you'll wear next week!

What You'll Need

- Pen, paper, and an envelope
- Camera

Step 1: Set Up

Check out the chart on the next page. You are going to record both qualitative and quantitative data that you think will affect what you will wear every day next week.

Step 2: Quantitative = By the Numbers - Week 1

Write down three quantitative facts that you think will affect what you will wear for each day next week.

Step 3: Qualitative = Feel it Out - Week 1

Think about all the social and emotional influences that will affect your outfit choices next week, then write down three qualitative facts that will affect how you dress each day next week.

Step 4: Fashion Your Plan - Week 1

Based on the data that you've recorded for each day, write down on a separate piece of paper what you think you will wear each day next week. Be as specific as you can! Then, fold up your paper, put it in your envelope, and seal it up. No peeking at your predictions!

Step 5: Selfie Heaven - Week 2

Go about your next week as normal. Each morning, just before you step out the door to start your day, take a picture of what you are wearing. If you've got a coat, jacket, or other top layer on, make sure to open it up so you can record what you're wearing underneath.

Step 6: The Envelope, Please - Week 3

Compare what you actually wore (take out those pictures!) with what you predicted you'd wear. What influenced the differences from your prediction? Was there an unpredicted change in the weather? Did you get sick, or land a hot date that made you want to wear something different? Did you have more quantitative or qualitative changes? Which changes were harder to predict, and why?

Game:
Fashion a Plan: Data Collection Worksheet

	Monday	Tuesday	Wednesday	Thursday	Friday
QUANT DATA	1. 2. 3.	1. 2. 3.	1. 2. 3.	1. 2. 3.	1. 2. 3.
QUAL DATA	1. 2. 3.	1. 2. 3.	1. 2. 3.	1. 2. 3.	1. 2. 3.

Game:
Bark vs. Purr: Which Do You PreFUR?

 2 Hours  2+ Players

Goal

Put your new research skills to the test by taking a stand for either cats or dogs. Which would you rather own? Pick your fave furry friend, and design the ideal toy for it. Then, convince an "investor" that your pet toy is the best bet for their funding.

What You'll Need

- Internet and/or library access
- Markers and a poster OR a collaborative space, such as a whiteboard or chalkboard

Step 1: Divide and Decide

Divide the group evenly into two teams. Designate one as Team Dog and the other as Team Cat. Choose one person to be the "investor." That person will not be a part of either team.

Step 2: Find Your Furry Focusing Statement

Referring back to the Sponge activity on focusing statements, come up with an improvement for your team's pet toy, by finishing this statement:
Team Cat: "I want to make play more _____ for cats."
Team Dog: "I want to make play more _____ for dogs."
Hint: Take a look at the current pet toys out there, and pick one aspect you'd like to make better.

Step 3: Spark Up a Solution

Spark three Solution Ideas for your Challenge statement. For example, if you wrote: "I want to make play more healthy for cats," perhaps you considered a tunnel with cat hair brushes on the inside walls. Pick just one Solution Idea for the next step.

Step 4: Make a Group Data Date

Research both qualitative and quantitative facts to support your solution. Consider the quality of your sources: A quote from a dog walker who works with different dogs all day long will be more convincing than a quote from a single-dog owner. Remember, you are collecting these facts to convince an investor to help turn your idea into a real product!

Step 5: Presentation Creation

Compile all your facts in one place. Add some fun visuals.

Step 6: Make Your Pitch

Each team must then present its solution to the "investor," who will pick one winning solution. Only one team can present at a time, without any interruptions from the other team. After the investor decides, discuss why that team won. Did they have more quantitative or qualitative data? Which type of data was more convincing?

Sparking a Solution Idea

You can Spark a good Solution Idea by asking a good set of thought-provoking questions that explore possibilities (with an understanding of the problem to ground them). In its IDEATE mixtape, Stanford's d.school came up with a great set of explorations they called HMW questions, for "How-Might-We?"

So, How-Might-We:

Amp up the good?

List the elements that are good in a situation and think of ways to make them even more positive. You could flip this and also ask, "How might we remove the bad?"

Use unexpected resources?

List the people, items, environmental factors, and other aspects of the context around your situation. How could they be used differently to help solve the problem?

Challenge an assumption?

In Sponge, we talked about assumptions that you may have about an activity, need, or group of people. List those on paper. Are there ways to challenge those assumptions, or work around them?

Your answer to these questions could be in the form of a creative action you that propose. and the thing you intend as the solution (more on those "things" in a moment). Some good action starters include:

Build, create, design, redesign, write, devise, compose, fabricate, fashion, form, invent, and produce.

Taking an example from page 35, if your problem is:
The track team's path crosses a busy roadway.

You could ask:
How might we amp up good?

Your exploration might lead to this thought:
Track practice is good in that it provides exercise. Can we find a solution that moves the path and provides more exercise?

And your Solution Idea may be:
Build an exercise obstacle course that directs track team members up and over the road rather than requiring them to cross it by walking. This leads to additional exercise and a clearer roadway.

Let's look at a case study that shows one path to a solution.

42

Spark Case Study: RunPee.com

In 2005, Dan Florio jumped out of his theater seat as the credits rolled. He had just spent over three hours watching Peter Jackson's movie *King Kong*, and spent the last 20 minutes of it urgently wishing that the ape would just die. Boy, did he have to pee.

As he passed the line of people waiting for the next showing, clutching their 64 oz. drinks, he wished he could tell them about a specific long, less-important scene in the middle of the movie. It was a perfect time to go pee, without missing anything they'd regret.

From this moment of urgent need and empathy for those people in line, Dan had a Spark. How might he remove the bad in watching movies in the theater? The bad was a full bladder. The solution: Find and share the best times to go to the bathroom. RunPee was born.

RunPee is a website and mobile app that provides suggested peetimes for blockbuster theatrical movies. Dan, his mother, his sister, and a movie reviewer watch new releases on Thursday and Friday nights and note the 3- to 5-minute sections of scenes that are missable, so that those who need to GO can do so without anxiety.

Are the plot developments easily summed up and low on the emotional scale? Peetime. Is this one of three car chases in the movie, and the least interesting? Peetime. Lots of exposition for things that you may already know from the first movie of the series? Peetime.

Dan and his team write up notes for those missable minutes and provide them to you, so you can catch up if you're using your phone during your short trip.

Dan recognized a need, felt empathy for others with that need, and proposed a solution that over 350,000 movie- (and restroom-) goers have used. The Solution Idea wasn't enough on its own, though. The design of the solution was key.

It's a Bit Viral

Dan doesn't pay for RunPee advertising. The idea is shared by word of mouth because it's quirky, easy to describe, and obviously useful for any film fan who feels the pain of long movies and big drinks.

How They Do It: Design and Content

Knowing that a bright mobile phone screen is not welcome in a dark movie theater, Dan designed the mobile app with a dark screen, and uses vibration to alert users to upcoming peetimes so they wouldn't have to constantly look at their phone.

As for the peetimes, and content such as the notes themselves, Dan and his team realized something else early on - the peetime expertise they provide is hard to copy.

You see, Dan originally thought to make the peetime information crowdsourced - meaning that users of the app could submit peetimes that others could refine and validate. More movies could be covered that way. But Dan found that the quality of user-generated information just wasn't high enough. He realized that there's a craft to choosing a good peetime.

Small children may be more willing to miss plot points than to miss action sequences, for example. An adult may not mind skipping part of a long action sequence as long as she doesn't miss major plot twists. Peetimes must be chosen wisely to have the right ones for the right movies and provide a good mix for different types of watchers.

Now, Dan and his team watch and enter all the movie information themselves. They realized that their understanding of the movie genre and audience is important to the value and quality of their solution.

Activity:
Striking a Spark

Using the case study you just read, fill out the rest of the Spark Frame below. Sketch if you'd like!

CHALLENGE		
Make this activity...	improved in this way (more, less...)	for these people:

SPARK	
Considering these problems...	Dan sparked his solution idea by asking:

SOLUTION IDEAS	
Dan's solution was...	Can you think of another?

Exploring Solutions

In our RunPee example, Dan chose to solve his problem by creating a digital product. That's a common type of solution, but it's not the only one. Let's use our dropoff problem from page 36 to illustrate different approaches.

Process solutions change the way people perform an activity. You could change the order of steps involved, add or remove steps, or change the timing. For example, maybe track practice could start earlier, or return to the gym for cooldown exercises to avoid the heaviest traffic.

People solutions add or subtract particular people or roles from a situation. Practice is over, so the track coach could act as a supervisor, temporarily rerouting traffic through the fire lane.

Product solutions add new products into the mix, which could be physical, digital, or both. (After all, digital products rely on a physical element, like a mobile phone.) This could include a bridge, catapult, digital signage, or something that tracks traffic patterns and sends an alert to an app when there's a backup.

Context solutions add changes to elements in the environment, like walkways or signs. Sometimes these involve product or process solutions, but with the characteristic of being fixed to a particular place at a particular time.

Some of the best overall solutions consider more than one of these solution types, because they often impact each other.

For example, if you add a product like a digital sign, you're affecting the context of the problem. What is the impact of that?

Also, if you decide to have the coach direct traffic, she may need a new process to help her determine when and how to direct the cars, and what to do if the fire lane is suddenly needed.

Activity:
Striking a Spark

Try using different sparks for the dropoff problem on p. 35 (combined with sketch on p.36.) Come up with three to five solutions to improve the situation. Consider changes of context, people, process, and product (or a combo). Challenge your assumptions. For example, maybe every parent doesn't need to drop off their own kid. Design a better carpooling process!

How might we amp up the good?

What's good now:

Solutions that amp it up:

_____

_____

_____

_____

How might we use unexpected resources?

Resources:

Solutions that use them:

_____

_____

_____

_____

How might we challenge assumptions?

Assumptions:

Solutions that challenge:

_____

_____

_____

_____

The Power of Infographics

Infographics are concise, visually engaging stories that present quantitative and qualitative info. Online, visual.ly has some examples.

For this challenge, you can sketch an infographic rather than creating a polished version. If you do want to create something digital, use tools such as PowerPoint, Keynote, Photoshop, or GIMP (free and available at gimp.org.)

To find photos, go to Flickr.com and use advanced search to find images that fall under the royalty-free Creative Commons license.

There are also online sources for free icon fonts like those at elegantthemes.com/blog/resources/elegant-icon-font.

THE SPARK CHALLENGE!

For your final chapter challenge, Spark some Solution Ideas for the project you explored in the Sponge challenge. You can create a new Challenge statement, as long as you get out in the field to sponge up information about the people you're designing for!

Use the two worksheets you'll see next, fill out your Challenge and Spark, and try to generate at least three possible Solution Ideas. Then, create an infographic or poster that represents your proposal and highlights your favorite idea of the three. The infographic on the facing page was created by Sprk'd (sprk-d.com) to explain the value of infographics. We like to go meta!

When you're done, you'll have a nice sketched or digital infographic that tells the story of your proposed solution, and the reason it's so important.

Level Up

If you're completing these activities with a group, use your infographic as the basis of a pitch for your solution.

Choose an impartial judge who has to choose to invest in one of the pitches! He or she should listen to each pitch and determine which one to invest in (with an explanation as to why).

WHY YOU NEED INFOGRAPHICS

90% of information transmitted to the brain is visual.

1/2 of the brain is dedicated to visual function.

90%

The eyes are a physical extension of the brain.

30x more likely
High quality infographics are 30 times more likely to be read than text articles.

12% faster
Publishers that feature infographics grow 12% faster than those that do not.

550k per month
The words "infographic" & "infographics" are searched 550,000 times per month.

HOW TO GET YOUR OWN SPRK'D INFOGRAPHIC

Initial meeting to discuss your needs & ideas

Sprk'd sends you a design brief, confirming direction

Submit a 50% deposit & our design elves start working their magic

10111000
10110110
01000011
We begin research or you can also supply us with data.

We send you a design(s) to review

You approve the design (up to two rounds of edits)

We deliver your shiny new infographic!

Pay the remaining 50%

Activity:
The Spark Frame

 5-15 Minutes 1+ Player

Fill out the Spark Frame below for your Challenge. You can fill out the Solution Ideas after brainstorming Sparks on the next page.

CHALLENGE		
Make this activity...	improved in this way (more, less...)	for these people:

SPARK	
Considering these problems...	we'll spark solution ideas by asking:
	Use the activity on page 47 to find sparks.

SOLUTION IDEAS		

Activity:
Striking a Spark

Use this worksheet to brainstorm solutions for your project's problems.

How might we amp up the good?
What's good now:

Solutions that amp it up:

_____

_____

_____

_____

How might we remove the bad?
What's bad now:

Solutions that remove it:

_____

_____

_____

_____

How might we use unexpected resources?
Resources:

Solutions that use them:

_____

_____

_____

_____

How might we challenge assumptions?
Assumptions:

Solutions that challenge

_____

_____

_____

_____

Challenges You Can Chew

Itchy for Info?

These are often good sources of (relatively) unbiased research:

- Federal government
- Provincial/state governments
- Statistics agencies
- Trade associations
- General business publications
- Magazine and newspaper articles
- Annual reports
- Academic publications
- Library sources
- Computerized bibliographies
- Syndicated services (such as the Associated Press)

Insane for Infographics?

Try using different infographic templates to represent the same data. Here's a list of free ones: http://www.hongkiat.com/blog/infographic-design-kit/

The Debrief

Are you proud of your poster?

It represents a lot of work and thoughtfulness! It's easy to underestimate the effort that can go into a grounded Solution Idea.

Sometimes people generate ideas based on gut instinct, but often they don't have the context to make a really great solution. If you just go with your gut, it can also be easy to ignore the positive results that come out of the existing situation and only focus on the negative. You want to keep the positive! (Or replace the positive with another kind of positive).

Now you not only have a great idea for something to design in the next step - you've also gained important context about the issue, insight into the people who encounter the problem you're solving. All that AND the data to show how important it all is!

PIE I WANT TO EAT

PIE I HAVE EATEN

NOM NOM NOM NOM

In the next chapter, we'll talk about taking a solution idea and generating a lot of design concepts for it in a short period of time. This is called Splatter because at this point you should just get them up on the wall (or in your notebook) without judging them too quickly. Let's mix the paints and get started!

Splatter!

You're About to:

Learn the language of your eyes

Solve a problem for bald heads

Redesign your bedroom

Dissect a corpse

Paper a wall with ideas

Did You Know?

Jackson Pollock was an artist who became well-known for his abstract art. In particular, he had a style of drip painting where he used splatters of paint dripped onto flat canvases.

To some, this kind of splatter art can seem random. But abstract artists like Pollock excel at creating forms and shapes that seem to have an underlying meaning. Our brains WANT to form patterns in things, whether they're splatters of paint on a canvas or the shapes of clouds in the sky. So splatter at random for a while, and see what your brain can make of it!

Have you ever tried to paint on a blank canvas? If so you may know that it's very hard to go from nothing to something that's beautiful, moving, or thought provoking.

It may seem like the great painters could naturally handle a blank canvas—that they just knew how to see things differently and paint amazing works. But when you go to an exhibition of artists like Pablo Picasso or Salvador Dali, you'll see that they spent a lot of time sketching variations of the forms they were about to paint.

Picasso himself ended up painting 58 versions of another painter's work (Las Meninas by Velazquez), to explore differences in style, color, and form! In Leonardo da Vinci's sketchbooks you can see several sketches of the same person's arm from slightly different angles, as well as concepts for flying machines that were centuries ahead of their time.

These artists knew one of the most important rules of design: To come up with something really different and impactful, you need to let yourself explore lots of possibilities. You need to open up your mind and express things, without the pressure of getting something right the first time that you put pen to paper. You need to splatter the paint for a while!

Then, when you have a lot of mess and color to look at, you'll see patterns and find inspiration that you never would have seen if you stuck with your first idea.

In this adventure you will learn how to take a Solution Idea like the ones you **SPARKED** in the last chapter, and quickly generate a lot of different concepts related to it. We call this SPLATTER because, like splattering paint, you don't worry too much about where it all lands - just get a bunch of ideas out in a visual way using techniques like sketching and posting up concepts. Once you have your concepts splattered on the wall or table, the patterns that you'll find can be very interesting!

Questions to Ponder:
- Why is a picture "worth a thousand words?"
- If sketching is so powerful, why don't people use it more often?
- Why should we spend any time talking about concepts that seem impossible to create?

What You'll Do:
- Try your hand at the basics of sketching and learn about its importance when you're generating ideas.
- Go big or go home. Then go big at home! Create a large number of concepts in a group challenge, then keep going for the next 24 hours.
- Learn how to find patterns in your splatter of ideas. Build on them or use them to splatter even more.

More on Concepts

Designers spend a lot of time generating and discussing concepts. A design concept is an idea that has not yet been fully developed into a product or service.

The concept can be something that exists only in your mind, or as a basic sketch on a piece of paper. It can also be a complete model of something that hasn't yet been made available to everyone, like a concept car.

For the purposes of our adventure, we'll be using basic sketches as concepts, like this concept for a puppy skateboard:

Why Designers Sketch Concepts

Sketching is a quick method for expressing ideas in a visual way, rather than just using words. But why is it so important to express information visually? Here are a few of the many reasons:

ANGRY GLARE

SODAS:
24oz or 64oz

海月

Go down the hallway and take your second right. It's the first door on your left, right before the water fountain.

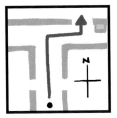

Some concepts, such as emotions, have more impact when expressed visually. Which of these two boxes seem to have a bigger impact on you?

Images can also be more effective at communicating such things as the relationships between objects, and their relative sizes.

Signs are designed to communicate regardless of which language you speak. If you were on the beach in Japan and considering a swim, which sign would you rather have?

Verbal directions are useful for step-by-step instructions, but the visual form is often easier to grasp at a higher level, or to understand your current location.

Verbal and visual information activates different sides of your brain. If you're not used to using both sides often, it can be difficult to get started. Let's try a game that will exercise your ability to transcend the verbal/visual divide!

Game:
Talk Sketchy to Me

Goal
Learn firsthand why a picture is worth a thousand words (or, in this case, at least 25!) by successfully getting your partner to guess the phrase you are drawing.

What You'll Need
- Pen & paper

Step 1: Choose Your Roles
Pick one person to be the artist, and another to be the guesser.

Step 2: Pick a Noteworthy Statement
The artist should flip to page 144 and pick a statement from the list. The person who is going to guess should NOT look at that list.

Step 3: Sketch Your Statement
The artist then begins to sketch that statement, using only pictures! That means no letters or numbers, but symbols - such as a star or a heart - are OK.

Step 4: Best Guessed
The guesser should immediately begin guessing words and phrases out loud to identify the full statement. If the guesser says a correct word, you may write it down at the top of the page. Each word guessed correctly can be written down in the correct order. Keep going until the guesser correctly says the entire statement out loud.

Step 5: Think Sketchy
What words were difficult to sketch? Which were easier? How did the artist use the paper to visually communicate how words related to each other? Can you isolate parts of the sketch where one image was able to capture several words?

Step 6: Replay Value
- Have a big group and want to play again? Have teams compete against each other to see who can get it right first. (Level up the challenge: Have each team write the statement for the opposing team.)

- Go digital: Play again but have the artist communicate solely through images found using Google Image Search.

Visual Language

In the fantastic book *Gamestorming*, by Gray, Brown, and Macanufo (O'Reilly Media, 2010), the authors write about visual language as a distinct skill unlike reading, writing, and arithmetic:

The authors go on to outline a basic visual vocabulary of 12 shapes from which all other shapes can be made:

Flow shapes are linear and can be linked together in a sequence. They include dot, line, angle, arc, spiral, and loop.

Closed shapes feel more like solid objects. They include oval, eye, triangle, rectangle, house, and cloud.

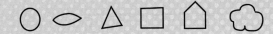

Try drawing the following using the shapes above. Don't worry too much about erasing!

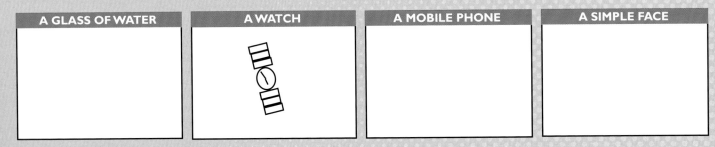

Sketching Many Concepts

Another reason that designers love sketching is because it's fast and cheap. With nothing more than a pencil and some paper, you can sketch many concepts of one Solution Idea. This kind of exercise is called "generative" because the goal is to generate a lot of different possibilities.

For example, if your Challenge is:
Make biking more luxurious for bald people

And your Solution Idea is:
Design a helmet that is safe and comfortable for those who are hairless

You could sketch three different concepts for a helmet, like:
- One with a sun-resistant screen
- One with a built-in wig
- One with slip-resistant rubber

Or you could sketch three different designs for one concept, such as three mullet styles for the built-in wig concept. Maybe you just concentrate on the design of the clasp for a while.

Sketching is collaborative. You can compare your sketches with those of others, or start a sketch and then pass it to someone else who adds to it. She may come up with an entirely different interpretation of where you were going!

Read the following case study and try your hand at creating multiple sketches.

Just Draw the Line

You say you can't draw? That stops a lot of people. Someone may think he'll be judged on his shaky lines, or may feel embarrassed when someone else thinks his cat is a horse.

Your drawing doesn't have to be perfect to do what it needs to do: represent an idea in a visual way. A simple smiley face is recognizable as a face. A stick figure represents a person. These are just circles, dots, and lines, but they're a very powerful form of shorthand.

You don't even have to represent something well enough to stand on its own. A sketch can help you explain concepts to others in person.

The Case of the Bald Biker

Nick, Leslie, and Ryan formed a team that was given the following design challenge:

Make biking more luxurious for bald people.

They broke up the Sponge step. Leslie did qualitative interviews with bald bikers. Ryan observed bald bikers in the wild. Nick did online research to understand current product offerings for bikers.

Then they shared their findings with each other. They found an important problem. Bald bikers were not happy with their helmets because:

- Many helmets are not solid caps, but have holes in the top for ventilation. These holes put the bald scalp at risk of sunburn. The more advanced the helmet, the more pronounced the issues were. The nicest helmet cost $180 and looked like swiss cheese.

- Many helments are padded with a foam which, when lubricated with sweat, makes it slip on a smooth head.

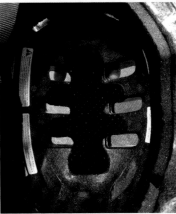

Activity:
The Bald Biker Spark Frame

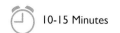 10-15 Minutes   1+ Player

Use the Case of the Bald Biker to fill out the rest of the Spark Frame below!

CHALLENGE		
Make this activity...	**improved in this way (more, less...)**	**for these people:**
Biking	more luxurious	Bald people

SPARK	
Considering these problems...	**we'll spark solution ideas by asking:**
	How might we make helmets more safe and comfortable against skin?

SOLUTION IDEAS		

Activity:
Bald Biker Sketch Challenge

Sketch three designs using the outlines below, and three more from scratch! Then compare yours with someone elses' if you can.

62

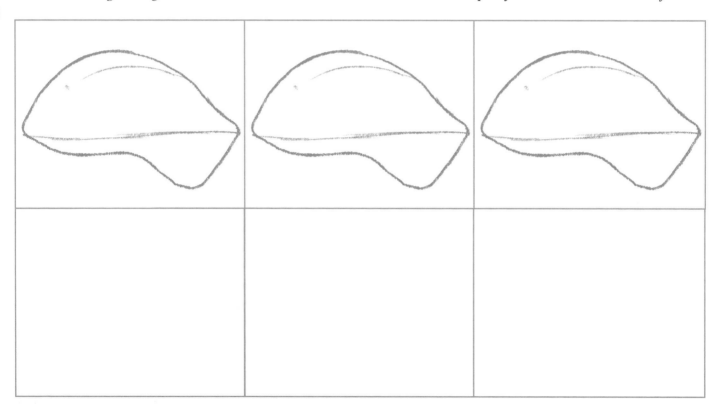

Activity:
An Alarming Digital Sketch Challenge

 5-10 Minutes   1 Player

Designers sketch for digital solutions as well as physical products. Try your hand at digital sketching below by drawing two different digital alarm clock interfaces for a handheld mobile device. Try to design a digital alarm clock that would make waking up less heinous for night owls:

TOUCH OWL TO SNOOZE

Did you enjoy digital sketching? If so, try to design a digital interface that would help our bald bikers plan for the day.

It's No Shame to Reframe

During your sketching, you may reach a point where the original Solution Idea just doesn't seem strong enough. Maybe something else you sketched made you think of another way to address the root cause of the problems.

You may even start to wonder if the "how might we" Spark you used to find a Solution Idea was really the right question to ask.

It's not unusual for this to happen. Thinking visually activates more of your mind, and it may connect to something from your previous field research that you didn't think of earlier.

Pay attention to this! The way you ask a question impacts the types of solutions you explore. It forms the frame of your solution, and sometimes the first frame you try doesn't end up fitting as well as it might.

Changing the question that you ask is called "reframing." It's a natural part of the design process. Let's say you wanted to make biking more luxurious for bald people, which led you to ask:

How might we make helmets more safe and comfortable against skin?

That question makes the assumption that you're working only with helmts. Reframe by asking:

How might we make helmets unnecessary?

This reframe might lead you to design a shock-triggered force field around the biker, or air bag sunglasses that inflate when the biker's head is about to hit something at high speed.

Reframing is an excellent technique for thinking even bigger. It helps you break out of current assumptions. Try writing three different sparks for our bald biker challenge.

Consider how we might:
- Amp up the good
- Remove the bad
- Use unexpected resources
- Challenge an assumption
- Look from a different person's point of view
- Use an analogy (How might we make biking like flying? Or student dropoff like an assembly line?)

These questions are from: IDEATE Mixtape, Stanford d.school - http://dschool.stanford.edu/wp-content/uploads/2012/02/ideate-mixtape-v8.pdf

Game:
Reframe in the Membrane

Goal

Brainstorm new possibilities by introducing unexpected and downright strange elements to your Spark Frame.

What You'll Need

- Pen & paper

Step 1: Refit Your Challenge

Write down your Challenge statement at the top of a piece of paper. You are going to modify that statement by adding a physical or contextual constraint. Pick one Object or Scenario.

Step 2: Generate a List

- If you picked Object, write down the first 25 objects that pop into your head. They can be anything: taco, cat, computer, fleas, etc.
- If you picked Scenario, write down the first 25 possible scenarios for the challenge that pop into your head. They can be digital, such as "on a mobile device"; physical, such as "at the drive-in movie theater"; or even completely unrealistic, such as "on a world with no gravity."

Step 3: Stretch Your Concepts

Referring back to your Challenge statement, retrofit it to include each term in your list, and quickly generate one to three ideas for the new Challenge. Be silly! Be weird! Have fun! For example, if your Challenge was: "Make going to the beach more fun for the easily sunburned," and your Object was "coat hanger," then maybe a concept is using the hanger as a DIY tent frame so pale-skinned beach-goers can relax in the shade, using their towel as a tent.

Step 4: Review Your Results

How did adding unexpected design constraints change the way you looked at your Challenge? Did you come up with any new concepts that you think might actually work?

More Ways to Play: For a Group

Pair people up and have partners generate the list of Objects or Scenarios for each other - without knowing the other player's Challenge, of course.

A Haiku for You

Have you ever written a haiku? It's a traditional Japanese poem that often has a constrained structure of:

- One line of about 5 sound units (simlar to syllables)
- One line of about 7 sound units
- One line of about 5 sound units

Doesn't sound like there's much room for creativity, does it? But the structure focuses writer and reader on the beauty of words.

Over the wintry
forest, winds howl in rage
with no leaves to blow.

– Natsume Soseki

Haikus illustrate another design principle: that less is more. Keeping things simple can make them more powerful - and more likely to be appreciated.

Working with Constraints

When you added new objects or scenarios to your Challenge in the Reframe game, you were basically adding constraints.

Constraints are limitations that affect what you can design. For example, if you want to design a vegetable garden for your backyard, you may be constrained to certain areas (or certain kinds of plants) due to the amount of sun they can get during the day. Or, if you want to design an app for CIA agents, you may be constrained by security procedures.

Constraints may sound like bad things, but they often can be helpful. Starting with a totally blank slate can be difficult - just ask a novelist about starting with a blank screen when she's beginning a new book!

Sometimes, adding constraints helps you start with a structure that you can work within. It helps you focus on a smaller set of possibilities, and can also help you reframe the question you're trying to answer.

We'll talk about how constraints help you simplify when we get to Sculpt. For now, let's explore how adding (or removing) constraints can help you generate a lot of different variations when you're trying to Splatter a lot of concepts.

Game:
Interior Design Your Life

Goal
Understand designing with constraints by rearranging your bedroom furniture to suit different needs.

What You'll Need
- Ruler
- Pen & paper
- Scissors

Step 1: Measure Up
Using a ruler or measuring tape, measure your bedroom. Then, converting feet to inches, draw your room proportionally on a piece of paper. So, an 10.5 foot by 6 foot room would be 10.5 inches by 6 inches on paper.

Step 2: Doors, Windows, Closets
Now, measure your doorways, closets, windows - and any other openings in the walls of your room. Convert those measurements from feet to inches, too. Then, mark that distance off in your room drawing, being careful to place them correctly.

For example, if you have a three-foot window on your six-foot wall, measure where that window begins (two feet in from the corner) before marking off the proportionate three-inch window space in your drawing.

Helpful Hint: For doors that swing into your room, don't forget to measure the length of the door along with its opening radius (see the example on the next page) - or else you might "arrange" yourself into your room with no escape!

Step 3: Furniture
Last but not least! Measure all your furniture, again converting feet to inches. Draw your furniture on a separate piece of paper and cut them out. So, if your bed is 6 foot by 4.5 foot, draw a 6 inch by 4.5 inch rectangle, and cut it out. If you want to get fancy, you can "decorate" your paper furniture with photos. If not, you still might want to label each piece so you don't forget what it represents.

Step 4: Constraints? No Complaints!
Arrange your furniture in your room drawing to mirror the way you currently have it placed in your room. How could you rearrange your room to make it more fun? More convenient? What if you had to add in a second bed for a roommate? What if you wanted to move all the furniture around to have a party? Play with your furniture without breaking a sweat!

What elements in your room take up the most space? How does that constraint affect how you want to rearrange your space for different purposes?

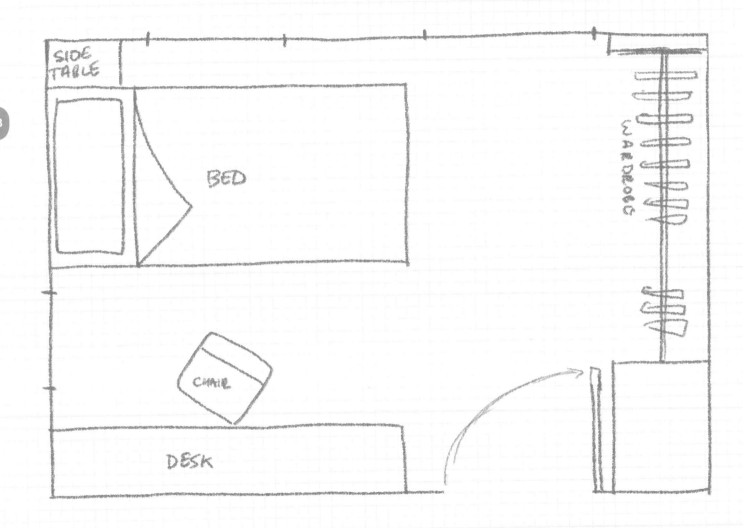

SIDE TABLE

BED

WARDROBE

CHAIR

DESK

Brainstorming Essentials

A generative brainstorm is a group discussion that's meant to generate or explore a lot of concepts in a relatively short period of time. You can then explore those concepts as a group to find interesting patterns. This is part of a process called *ideation*, which we'll be doing for the rest of Splatter.

Brainstorms work well when:

1. There's a clear goal to be accomplished.

For example, generate at least 20 concepts for a helmet solution.

2. There's a good set of questions or constraints to prompt ideation.

Like our How Might We questions on page 64.

3. Someone takes the role of facilitator.

It's a great skill to have! See Facilitation Tips for more.

4. Everyone is dedicating their time and attention.

No mobile phones or multitasking!

5. The tone of the discussion is open and playful.

During idea generation, no ideas are wrong, or too crazy.

6. You take time to build on ideas and detect patterns.

Look at the problem in multiple ways. Reframe, add, or remove constraints.

We've explored the first few points already. Let's dive deeper into the last two.

Facilitator Tips

Good facilitation skills will help you in almost any profession. Facilitation takes practice, but it's worth it! If you're facilitating:

- Choose a good open space with walls for putting up sketches.

- Bring the goal with you and state it clearly at the beginning.

- Have more questions and constraints in your "back pocket" to prompt people if they get stuck. Encourage quantity of ideas over quality.

- If someone in your group seems to be dominating the discussion, ask quieter folks for their opinions whenever there's a lull.

- Try to stay unbiased. You'll have time to Sculpt later!

Be Open and Playful

Every day, multiple times a day, you're faced with needs and making judgments about ways to address them.

Let's say you're trying to decide how to get to work during the summer. The bias you'll most likely have is for ways that are familiar, real, or feasible. If you usually take the bus, that's your most likely course. If the weather is nice, maybe you'll walk. You're not very likely to decide to fly because that's probably not feasible–unless you can fly or pay someone else to fly you!

When you brainstorm, it's OK to start by saying you'll fly to work. The point is to explore possibilities that may not usually occur to you. Jet packs? Mini-helicopters? Hovercrafts? These things aren't available now, but someone out there is trying to design them. As you heard in Spark, we didn't get cars by redesigning horses!

A good generative brainstorm is open to ideas that may seem silly. When you feel the judging part of your brain saying "that'll never work," "that makes no sense," or "this idea is a waste of time," just shut it off. Give the rest of your brain permission to play.

Your Spark is a focus for generating a lot of different ideas, and some of them *should* seem silly or crazy. That's how you get a wide set of ideas to work from. You open up a lot of different concepts and explore them (as you can see in A in the diagram below, from *Gamestorming*). Later, in Sculpt, you'll close in on part B - the concepts to focus on.

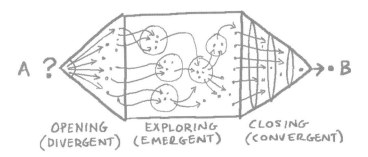

Let's try some games to open your brain!

Game:
Brainstorm Warm-Up: Shoe Tie, Shoe

 30 Minutes   1+ Player

Goal
Approach a need from several different angles by lacing your shoe in as many different ways as you can!

What You'll Need
- A shoe (unlaced) and a shoelace
- Pen & paper

Step 1: Investigate the Standard
Lace your shoe in the typical manner (crossing laces above and below where the two sides meet.) What are the benefits and disadvanages of this process? Write them down.

Step 2: Mix It Up
Now unlace and re-lace your shoe in as many different ways as you can think of. Each time you lace it, draw a quick sketch of your approach and write down some of the pros and cons of lacing your shoe that way.

Step 3: Think It Through
Were any of the lacing methods that you came up with better than the standard method? Why do you think most people lace up their shoes the way they do?

Feeling Competitive?
If you've got a group, set the timer for 30 minutes and see who can come up with the most ways to lace a shoe. Compare everyone's results at the end: What similar methods did people try? Why do you think that was? What unique methods did the winners come up with? Why did no one else think of the winners' lacing options?

Added Challenge
Try to lace and tie shoes in as many different ways as you can using any material you can find or think of, from wire to an iPhone cord... What works?

Game:
Brain Cardio: The Game of Phones

Goal

Stuck on one concept? This brainstorm technique is designed to illustrate how even one message can be expressed in a cornucopia of ways.

Step 1: Establish a Connection

Determine a linear order for all the players. Sit in a line or other configuration that clearly begins with one player and ends with another player.

Step 2: Send a Message

Player one gets the honor of choosing a one-sentence message. Try to use colorful and descriptive adjectives.

Step 3: Scramble the Airwaves

Just as in the game of Telephone, player one will whisper her message to player two, who will whisper the same message to player three, and so on until you get to the final player, who will relay the message out loud for everybody to hear. (For those of you unfamiliar with Telephone, try to keep the message a secret as it is transferred via whisper from player to player. And no repeating the message if you don't hear it right the first time!)

Unlike Telephone, however, players in The Game of Phones will actively try to alter the wording of the message without altering its content. For example, if the message is, "The bird is blue," then player two might pass on the message, "The winged beast is blue." Player three might evolve that further to: "The winged beast is azure."

Step 4: Uh, Operator?

When the message gets to the last player, she must also tweak it to be a little different before repeating it to the group. Did the meaning survive? How did the message transform? Did the words become more general, or more specific?

Game:
Boss-Level Brainstorming: "Exquisite Corpse"

Goal
Open your mind to unexpected sources of inspiration through collaborative sketching.

What You'll Need
- A sheet of paper for every player
- Markers and pens for everyone to sketch with
- A timer

Step 1: Pick a Theme
As a group, select a Challenge statement. This will be the theme of your brainstorm. Everyone will be sketching potential solutions to this Challenge.

Step 2: Sketch your Corpse!
Everyone in the group should start off with a clean sheet of paper in front of them. Set the timer for five minutes. During that time, everyone must sketch a potential solution to the Challenge statement. Draw in a corner of your sheet of paper. When you are done, you will be folding the paper over so that no one can see what you drew.

When the timer is up, everyone gets two minutes to add a title or line of text to their drawing. For example, if the

Challenge statement you picked was, "Make brushing your teeth more fun for kids," you might sketch a brush that plays music only when it is being used. Over that, you could write your favorite song lyric, coming from the toothbrush. Fold over the paper, so that all you can see is the text, and none of the drawing.

Step 3: Get Exquisite
Once everyone has folded over their paper, switch papers! Now, you must sketch a potential solution to the Challenge statement that also incorporates the text that you can see from the folded-over sketch. Repeat Steps 2 and 3 until there's no more space to sketch on the paper.

Step 4: Dissect your Corpse!
Completely unfold all the corpses and pin them up around the room so that everyone can check them out! What assumptions did people make about each other's copy?

Surrealist Brainstorming! Did you know?
The game Exquisite Corpse is based on a game called Consequences, which was a favorite of Surrealist artists like Salvador Dali. The game can also be played with just words. Just adhere to the sequence adjective, noun, verb. Each player writes down one word, then folds over the paper and passes it to create a very strange - sometimes surreal - story!

Detecting Patterns

When you have a lot of different concepts to look at, they may initially seem unrelated. But if you start moving them around, you may may see invisible connections that link some of them into groups. Sometimes you may find more than one set of connections among those groups. Each kind of meaningful grouping forms a pattern.

Designers will often put their ideas up on a wall on sticky notes. They do this so they can move each one around and see how they relate to each other. New connections form patterns that they can build on and add more detail to. This is why the "sticky wall" approach works well when looking for patterns among individual ideas or sketches created during a brainstorm.

Some ideas may be tackling a particular part of the problem to solve with a product solution. Still others may try to fix something else in the process (see page 46). Maybe there's a strong trend towards solutions available on a mobile phone that you discuss and build on.

Here's a simple exercise in pattern-finding.

Cars	Birds	Police Officers
Clowns	Boats	Fishermen
Lions	Criminals	Tuna
Planes	Piranha	Butterflies

At first look, the terms above may seem unrelated. But if you start moving them around, you'll start seeing connections. Let's say you move the following terms together in a group - what connection do they have?

1. Birds, Lions, Butterflies, Tuna, and Piranha

_____

2. Planes, Birds, Butterflies

_____

3. Police Officers & Criminals   Fishermen & Tuna

_____

4. Clowns, Criminals, Lions, Piranha

Things that Carolyn is afraid of
_____

What other patterns can you make with these terms?

Game:
Pick a Peck of People Patterns

Goal

Practice detecting patterns after brainstorming design concepts with a group.

What You'll Need

- A pad of sticky notes
- Pen

Step 1: Pick a Challenge

As a group, choose a Challenge. You can refer back to your results from the Sponge activity, or you can make up a new one. We recommend, "Make tacos less messy for children to eat."

Step 2: Hand out the Sticky Notes

Give each of the players the same number of sticky notes. Nine is a pretty good number to start with.

Step 3: Design Solutions

Without talking or consulting each other, everyone must come up with as many different design concepts as they can in the time allotted to address the Challenge. Write or sketch one concept per Post-It note.

Step 4: Sort Results

One by one, go around the room and have each player present his concepts. After each concept is explained, stick it on a board or wall that everyone can see.

Place similar concepts near to each other. As a group, discuss where to put each concept. Using the taco example from Step 1, you might place all concepts that revolved around re-designing the taco shell into one group. Name each group. In the case of our example, we'd call it "taco shells."

Don't be afraid to rearrange groups and further sub-divide as you go! For example, you might find that within the taco shell ideas, some people tried to create containers, while other redesigned the taco shells to replace utensils.

Step 5: The Big Picture

After you've plotted all of the concepts, step back and look at the patterns that emerged. What group is the biggest? Which is the smallest? Why do you think that some groups were bigger than others? After the brainstorm is over, keep sketching more concepts on your own over the next day. How are those concepts different?

THE SPLATTER CHALLENGE!

For your final chapter Challenge, hold a generative brainstorm and find patterns among the concepts you create.

Ideally, brainstorm with a group of three to six people and have one person take on the role of a facilitator. Try this multiple times with different Challenge statements, to give everyone a chance to facilitate!

What to bring:

- Use the Spark Frame you created at the end of the Spark chapter.
- Have someone bring at least two constraints and two Spark questions (or everyone can bring just one).
- Have sketch paper, sticky notes, pens, paper, and tape on hand so you can post your ideas.

Go somewhere quiet where you can spread out and put things up on the wall to see the big picture and find patterns. Use Brainstorm Fuel on page 77 to get started.

For timing, consider spending:

5 minutes going over your Spark Frame and making sure everyone knows how you developed it, and what you're trying to do.

5-10 minutes individually sketching concepts for one Solution Idea in your Spark Frame. Sketch as many concepts as you can in that time.

5 minute blocks to sketch concepts for EACH constraint and each Spark question. (So if you have two of each, that will take 20 minutes total.)

10 minutes to go around and have everyone explain their concepts and put them up on the wall.

10-20 minutes to group concepts and identify patterns while working together. Feel free to group and regroup, discussing the importance of each pattern you find.

Going it Alone?

You'll get a broader set of concepts by working in a group, so don't be shy in asking people (family members, friends, or other folks you know) to spend a lunch hour sketching with you!

If you do end up solo, give yourself a bigger set of constraints and Sparks. Be silly and think big! Carry your sketchbook around with you and use everything you see as inspiration, then go to the wall.

Brainstorm Fuel

Write these down before you start sketching concepts (and to add during):

Constraints	Spark Questions
_____	_____
_____	_____
_____	_____
_____	_____

After sharing your concepts, capture patterns here.
Consider the types of solutions that you're tending toward (people, process, context, and product), the problems you're trying to solve, and the areas of opportunity that seem to be of most interest.

_____

_____

_____

_____

_____

Spark Summary:

We want to make this activity:

_____

improved in this way:

_____

for these people:

_____

who have these problems:

_____

_____

We're exploring this solution:

_____

_____

For a full SPARK statement, see the example on page 30 or use the template on page 45.

78

The Debrief

Phew! We hope you had fun. Brainstorming is best when it involves play, but it also gets your mind working (think of it as plerking). That's why it's best to have a session when everyone's open and ready. If your brain hurts, treat yourself to something relaxing. You've earned it!

Now you should have identified a large number of concepts, and the interesting relationships between them. Some concepts may seem like something you could do today. Others may seem like a dream. You may love each and every one of them, but you're going to have to focus on a few and leave some of them behind (or at least, set them aside for now).

You're about to get even more real. In the next chapter we'll talk about validating design concepts to figure out which ones you should continue to work on. You'll winnow down these ideas to a few of the best, then visualize them with more refined sketches, and possibly a physical model! The key is to create something that you can give to the people you're designing for, to test your concept. That's what it means to SCULPT your concepts. It's time to trim!

Sculpt!

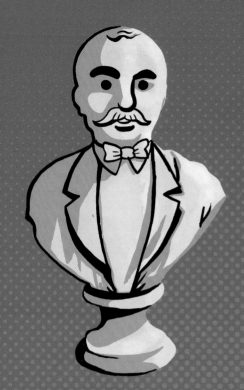

You're About to:

Make the best of a musical fest

Solve a problem for the unicorns of the ocean

Cook up a better date night

Sketch a solar-powered backpack

Find forms in foam core

Did You Know?

Clay is one of the first materials used for creating sculptures, but an amazing variety of substances have followed. Glass, metal, even trash and ice have been used to make great works of art.

Clay is especially effective when creating initial forms, or prototypes, that you can refine by adding and cutting away material. Once the clay sculpture looks right, it becomes the pattern for the molds that will help reproduce the form in a hardier substance. In this chapter, you'll cut, add, refine, and mold your concept until it becomes something more robust!

Have you ever noticed that two or more movies with the same basic plot often come out at the same time? Why does this happen?

Occasionally, something engages the attention of a large percentage of the world's population. Moviemakers notice this, and ideas for movies follow. A previously untracked comet came close to the earth in 1996, inspiring two movies - *Deep Impact* and *Armageddon* - which came out within two months of each other. Mayan predictions that the world would end in 2012 contributed to the enormous number of movies with "end of the world" themes such as *Seeking a Friend for the End of the World, 2012,* and *The World's End* (among others).

Designers, like moviemakers, track events or trends that have the attention of potential audiences - because they suggest concepts that audiences may find desirable. But sketching a good concept based on "what's hot" isn't enough to ensure a successful movie or a successful design. Those basic concepts need to be detailed and sculpted by a strong creative vision to inspire loyalty among their users and encourage repeat usage (or viewings.)

Like a scene from a well-made movie, each feature of a solution should be well chosen and meticulously crafted to provide an experience that's useful, delightful, and achievable with the technology and business resources at hand. Sometimes that even means saying no to some great ideas - but making those hard choices only clears the way for the right approach.

Try it yourself. It's time to Sculpt!

In this adventure you'll look at a broad range of concepts like those you generated in **SPLATTER**, and choose which ones to focus on and refine. This process is called **SCULPT** because, like a sculptor, you'll start by removing big chunks (or groups of concepts), and then refine what you have left by molding, adding, or cutting away features.

Questions to Ponder:
- What's easier? Adding a new feature to a product that people are using, or removing a feature that already exists?
- If people desire a particular concept, what barriers may exist that could stop that concept from being developed?
- Can you mimic the use of something with only a sketch?

What You'll Do:
- Explore the context in which a solution may be used.
- Create and apply your own design principles.
- Learn how to say no to unworthy concepts.
- Refine your design.
- Make a prototype and test it with others.

Yes AND, No BECAUSE

When you're brainstorming in the Splatter stage, it's helpful to build on the ideas of others with a trick used by improv comedians. When your partner says something like, "Did you see that kangaroo hopping by?" respond with "YES, AND it was wearing a birthday hat!" rather than saying "NO" and leaving your partner to come up with the next possibility.

In Sculpt, you eventually need to start saying NO. But the way to avoid leaving your partners hanging is by having good, solid reasons for your no. Find the BECAUSE by asking the questions throughout the following pages.

The Power of a Savvy No

It may seem that the most difficult part of design is coming up with ideas for solutions, concepts, and features. But professional designers will tell you that knowing when to say "no" to a concept, or a particular feature, is really tough - and getting your whole team to agree is even tougher!

Why is it so difficult to say no? Here are some reasons:

- Creation is a personal and gratifying activity that can make you feel strongly attached to your ideas. Saying no means walking away from something that feels like part of you.
- A valued team member may have had the idea and you don't want to disappoint or contradict them.
- The concept that you're saying no to addresses a genuine need that you or a team member finds important. It's hard to prioritize.
- If you're redesigning a solution that already exists, you might think that the people you're designing for will miss the feature you're removing.

Sounds difficult! But don't worry. You've said no already. You said it in Spark and Splatter when you chose just one solution to present or brainstorm.

The challenge now is to find a Savvy No.

A Savvy No is a decision that's based on consistent intentions and objective information. For example, you could base your decision on:

- Research you've conducted with users (as you did in Sponge)
- Constraints you need to work with (as we discussed in Spark)
- Design principles and standards that you choose for your solution
- The context in which your solution will most likely be used
- Your available resources and technology (called *feasibility*)
- The idea's business value (called *viability*)

We've talked about the first two sources for a Savvy No - let's take a closer look at the rest!

Game:
Saying No Like a Pro

 10 Minutes per round

 3+ Player

Goal

Sculpting ain't easy, but some people - such as news editors - do it every day. Practice making tough sculpting decisions with this newspaper game.

What You'll Need

- Simultaneous Internet access for all players
- Pens & paper
- Timer

Step 1: All Hail to the Editor in Chief

Imagine that you're on the staff of a national newspaper. Select one person to be Editor, and everyone else is a reporter. Each reporter must select a "beat" - a subject matter that he or she will report on, i.e. international news, sports, crime, education, arts, etc.

Step 2: Prep the Printing Press

Cut a piece of paper into strips so that each reporter has a piece large enough to write down their beat and a headline.

Step 3: Hot Scoop! (5 minutes)

Editor, start your timer! Your reporters have five minutes to comb the Internet, newspaper, and any other current sources to find the most important story of the day on their beat. When the time is up, each reporter must write a headline on their strip of paper.

Step 4: The Front Page Kerfuffle

The editor must now collect the headline strips and build a front page by placing the headlines in order from most important to least important. Reporters: Argue why your headline should be the top news story of the day! Editor: Act in the best interest of your readership. Imagine that your audience is the same age as you are. Consider which stories are most important for your audience and why, and then use that reasoning to support your editorial decisions. The reporter who brings in the top news article gets one point; the second article gets two points, and so on.

Step 5: News Cycle

Play again and take turns until everyone has had the opportunity to act as the Editor. To mix up the news headlines, the Editor should pick a different day of that month from which the reporters select headlines. Don't forget to keep track of points! The player with the lowest point total wins.

Did more than one Editor use the same reasoning in picking the lead headline for the day? What were some of the common themes among the headline rankings? The justifications for these decisions are called design principles. Let's take a closer look at how design principles can help you Sculpt your Solution Ideas.

Design Principles

Design principles are guiding statements that set the standard for what you're going to create. They help you make choices at all levels - from Solution Ideas, to concepts, to features - and say no to ideas that may have low impact.

Your principles can be based on your user insights, interesting patterns you found during Splatter, or an understanding of your solution's context of use. You can use these principles to choose a Solution Idea, to rule out concepts, or to prioritize features.

For example, here are the three Solution Ideas we considered when planning *Adventures in Experience Design* (page 30):

1. **Develop a video game that requires individuals to design their way out of a sticky situation.**

2. **Host a design challenge event staffed by volunteer designers.**

3. **Write a book that uses activities and games to explain design practices.**

We chose these design principles for our solution:

- Our creation should be highly repeatable for both individuals and groups. (You can easily use the games and activities multiple times, with different Challenge statements.)
- It can be used with low-cost materials so that it's more accessible for students.
- Activities should be relevant to real projects.

You could take these principles and make them even more memorable by writing them like this:

- Repeatable Process
- Accessible Play
- Real-Life Relevance

Using these principles, we ruled out the design challenge event (2) because we knew it would be tough to repeat it in every city, multiple times. And we ruled out the video game because it requires a computer or mobile device, which compromised our principle of "Accessible Play."

The video game also didn't fit one of the main "contexts of use" we were targeting: classrooms. Let's talk more about context of use, which ultimately helped us choose our design principles.

Activity:
The Principles' Office

Looking back at Splatter, write down three solutions you considered for the Spark Frame from your final challenge.

For example: Creating a video game to teach experience design.

_____

_____

_____

Now, think about the criteria you used to evaluate those Solution Ideas. A good place to start is to ask what attracted you to those solutions in the first place (such as findings from research). These are your design principles. Write them down below:

Video games are fun, because they teach experiences by putting the user into a story.

_____

_____

_____

Finally try to boil down those design principles into phrases of two to ten memorable words.

Immersive, Personal Lessons

_____

_____

_____

Context Questions

Answering these questions will help you envision context when designing:

- Where will this solution be used most often?
- What will people be doing?
- Will they be interrupted frequently?
- What kind of space will they have available?
- Will anything restrict their movements? How about their sight, hearing, touch, smell, or balance?
- How long will they need to use this solution? Is it used during a course of multiple activities, or in one short activity?
- Will users be with other people? If so, how might others become involved?

Context of Use

When you went out to observe people in Sponge, you chose to meet them in a particular context. Maybe it was their workplaces, their homes, or some other places in-between.

The context doesn't include just the place itself, but also several things that affect a person's actions or thoughts at a particular time. Think of how a bus differs for the driver and the passengers.

	BUS DRIVER	PASSENGER
I am here... environment	On a moving bus	On a moving bus
I'm in the middle of... activity	Driving Finding & picking up passengers	Paying my fare Finding a seat, or pole to hold on to Filling the time
I have to pay attention to... attention	Other vehicles & pedestrians The "Stop Requested" signal Who has and hasn't paid	The nearness of my stop The strangers around me My belongings (pickpockets!)
I'm here with... company	No one except passengers	No one except strangers & driver Co-workers Friends
I'm limited because... constraints	I need both hands to drive I can't drive with headphones	I'm holding on to a pole with one hand It may be too loud to talk easily

If you were designing a system that warned a bus driver when someone hasn't paid the fare, you'd have to create a design principle like "Free Hands & Ears." What other principles come to mind?

Activity:
Sketch Challenge: Context of Use

  45 Minutes   1+ Player

Imagine that you are designing a mobile app for an outdoor summer music festival. Consider how the various people described on this page might experience a music festival, and sketch the many different contexts in which they'd use their mobile phones.

Concert Goer/Music Fan

First Aid Tent Medic

Music Performer/Roadie

Food or Souvenir Seller

If you've ever been to a crowded music festival, you probably have experienced the frustration of poor phone reception due to an overloaded network. It's important when defining the context of use to also consider potentially less-than-ideal circumstances in a situation.

Feasibility, Viability, Desirability

During these adventures, you may not have been too focused on what's actually possible to create. This is called "Blue Sky Design" because you ignore the stormy clouds of reality for a while. If you're working on a real-world project, though, you're going to need to consider the *feasibility* and *viability* of your ideas. These sculpting factors, plus desirability, are three pillars of how to innovate through design (introduced by Tim Brown of design firm IDEO).

FEASIBILITY

Feasibility is the ability to actually create your design with the technology that's available today, or in the very near future.

Leonardo da Vinci is famous for sketching visions of flying machines centuries before the Wright brothers had their first successful flight. Visions like his are important to realize larger change! If you want to create something quickly, however, you'll need to choose concepts that can be created with technology you have at hand, or with technology that has a good chance of being developed soon (perhaps with your own concept as a motivation.)

> **Questions that help you determine feasibility:**
>
> Are solutions out there today already using the components you need to make this happen?
>
> If not, are those components in the works (in the news, for example, as being available in the next few months)?

VIABILITY

The technology could be possible, but can your concept be developed and used in a way that supports a business goal? This doesn't necessarily mean that your idea has to make money, but it has to help reach a goal that has value to whoever develops the concept, such as growing customer loyalty or improving student test scores.

Product solutions obviously have a cost of development, but so do process or people solutions (if you have to pay someone to develop it, or be trained in the new process).

If you're creating something that makes no money and has no business value, be prepared to either do it for personal practice, or out of a love for the concept!

> **Questions that help you determine viability:**
>
> How much do you think it would cost to develop your concept?
>
> Will the solution itself make money? (For example, will you charge for it?) If not, what other value may offset the cost?

Desirability

Desirability is the third pillar of innovative design. It's the human element. Do people feel a need for your solution? Will it make an obvious difference in their lives? Is it better than what's available elsewhere?

Watching people use competitive solutions is a great way to find out what they like and dislike, and to find to find the gaps that may exist in how their needs are being being addressed. Just be careful not to get stuck in the trap of copying your competitors. You'll need to be different, and better!

Your stiffest competition may actually be a solution that people are using today, even if your idea seems superior. There's a cost for people to switch from one solution to another. Sometimes it's money, but it's often the time and effort it takes to learn how to use something new. Why should people bother to change to your way of doing things?

> **Questions that help you determine desirability:**
>
> How urgent is the need you're addressing? Or, how urgent do you think it will seem once a better solution comes along?
>
> Is there an obvious gap in how well the need is currently addressed?
>
> Is there an opportunity to reframe the question so that you're not directly competing, but offering an entirely different way to meet your users' needs? (We discussed reframing on page 64.)

All right, let's put these sculpting tools to work! Read the following case study, along with information on related problems and the people who are encountering them. Then choose the concept you think is best, based on factors such as context of use, feasibility, viability, and desirability.

Contrast & Compare

Competitive solutions are important to consider, but it's interesting to explore *comparative* solutions - those that are not directly related but represent an interesting model that helps you make connections.

Think about Amazon.com's design for book recommendations (those who bought the book you're looking at, also bought this...). How might you apply this concept when creating a digital map of a museum?

Sleepin' with the Fishes, Sea?

The managers of the Nemo Maritime Aquarium are at their wits' end. A large amount of money was spent on building a new pool for a temporary narwhal exhibit, opened just last month. No narwhals have been successfully kept in captivity, in any country, but a rescued narwhal and her new baby are undergoing four months of treatment before being released. It's a rare and limited opportunity to see the toothed whales.

After an initial rush of narwhal enthusiasts, the number of ALL visitors has dropped off dramatically - by 30%! Something has to be done.

The managers ask you for help. You decide to observe visitors, stopping some to ask them about their experiences. You find visitors are frustrated with crowd congestion, caused in part by the following problems:

International visitors often come as part of a tour group, and can't easily read the English-only signs. As a result, they often stand in the wrong ticket line, and get lost when trying to find the narwhal exhibit.

Those who are visiting mainly to see the narwhals have to walk through general use space, thereby adding to the crowds.

Make the aquarium less congested by designing a better system for groups visiting the narwhals.

Choose a concept on page 93, using the context provided.

Constraints

- Non-paying visitors need to be able to enter the gift shop and cafeteria without buying a ticket.
- The narwhal exhibit ticket requires a general admission ticket also, but general admission does not have to include a narwhal ticket.
- The cost of developing your concept should be lower than the ticket revenue loss currently projected (about $60,000 total, over the remaining three months of the exhibit)

Design Principles

- Focus people on the exhibits, not the path to them.
- Encourage exploration of all exhibits.
- Don't make things worse for non-group visitors.
- Make sure the solution is repeatable for future special exhibits.

Sleepin' with the Fishes, Sea?

MAP

91

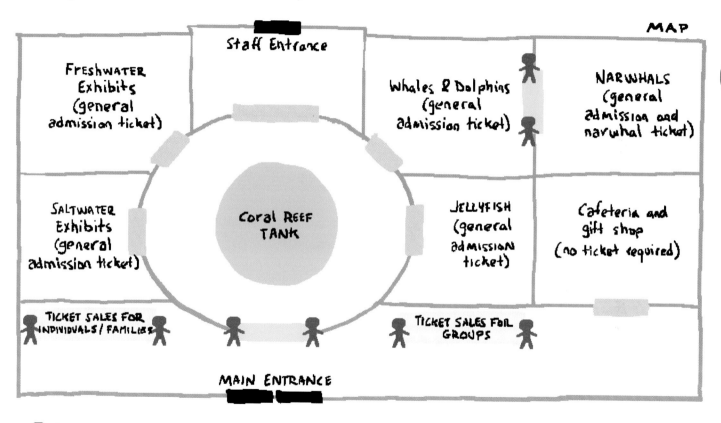

Staff Entrance

Freshwater Exhibits (general admission ticket)

Whales & Dolphins (general admission ticket)

NARWHALS (general admission and narwhal ticket)

Coral REEF TANK

Saltwater Exhibits (general admission ticket)

JELLYFISH (general admission ticket)

Cafeteria and gift shop (no ticket required)

TICKET SALES FOR INDIVIDUALS / FAMILIES

TICKET SALES FOR GROUPS

MAIN ENTRANCE

 STAFF MEMBER

 LOCKABLE DOOR

OPEN ARCHWAY

TICKET-CONTROLLED ARCHWAY (REQUIRES AT LEAST 2 STAFF MEMBERS)

Sleeping with the Fishes: Personas

TRAVELING JOAQUÍN

Personal Information

Age: 20 years old

Joaquín is a college student from Ecuador who is working as an assistant tour guide for the summer. Today he's helping his group visit the narwhal exhibit. His boss knows English well, but Joaquín has difficulty with words that he doesn't encounter every day.

Goals

- Travel the world, and see things he may never get another chance to see - like a real narwhal!
- Guide the members of his group to the right place quickly, with minimal confusion. He wants to be good at his job.

Frustrations

- When areas are crowded, Joaquín may lose track of some of his group members. He ends up wandering around to find them, and they become frustrated.
- It can be difficult to find specific areas within places like the aquarium. The signs aren't always clear, and paths aren't as straightforward as they could be.
- Every time the group has to go through a line, it's a lot of work for him. He wishes there was a way to avoid lines altogether.

MUSEUM MEREDITH

Personal Information

Age: 36 years old

Meredith is the mother of two: a three-year-old girl, and a seven year old boy. Every month, she takes her kids to a different museum in the area. They won't have time to see all of the exhibits, so she has to prioritize.

Goals

- Introduce her children to new experiences, expanding their knowledge of the natural world.
- Feel comfortable and safe, so she can focus more on the exhibits and her children, rather than directions and crowds.

Frustrations

- When areas are crowded, Meredith worries about keeping track of both of her children. They tend to wander off in different directions!
- Meredith doesn't like paying upfront for things she may not use. If she could make her decision to pay for narwhal tickets near the end of the visit, when she knows whether or not they'll have time, she may do it. But she thinks it'll be more of a hassle than it's worth to get to the right the ticket area and wait in line.

Activity:
Sleepin' with the Fishes, Sea?

 30 Minutes 1+ Player

Which concept below do you think would be best to develop to meet the challenges outlined on page 90.

Group Migration

Replace the staff entrance with a group ticket counter. Hire someone to direct groups to that side of the building.

Doors & Docents

Build a new archway between the cafeteria and narwhals, staffed by two new docents (guides) who check tickets.

Air Tube

Build an air tube that transports narwhal ticket holders directly from the lobby to the narwhal exhibit.

I Saw the Signage

Create new signs throughout the aquarium that are appropriate for international visitors (about 150 signs).

Why is your chosen concept the best? Do you have a better one? Consider context of use, design principles, feasibility, viability, and desirability. Research the costs that may be involved, such as the average salary of a museum staff member.

_____

_____

_____

Concepts vs. Features

In Spark, you generated ideas for solutions, and in Splatter, you sketched out many concepts for a chosen solution.

In Sculpt, you are detailing your ideas for features - the details within a chosen concept. Here's how they're related:

Solution
Design a better helmet for bald people

Concept
A helmet with attachable wig

Features
- "No-pinch" chin clasp
- Racing stripe
- Wind guard
- Multi-snap wig system
- Moisture-wicking wig hair
- Five different exchangeable wig styles

Now Featuring... Features!

A large part of desirability isn't just the solution behind your concept, but the details of your concept's design - the way it looks and feels, the features included, and how a person goes about using it (his interaction with it). If you design a product that people enjoy using and feel proud to own, they're likely to spread the word to others. But if your concept is weighed down with too many competing features, people may feel the effort to learn it isn't worth the time.

Think of features as the building blocks of a concept, each of which has an inherent, independent value (although many will be more valuable or usable when grouped together). How you choose and prioritize the features of your concept is an important part of the design process.

Let's say you had chosen to address our narwhal challenge by creating a digital product - a mobile app that helps guide a person to the exhibits she'd like to visit. There are basic features, or requirements, that represent the minimum functionality that you need to include. You could say that a user of this app must be able to:

- Download information specific to the museum she's visiting (in this case, the aquarium.)
- Browse the exhibits that are currently available to view at that museum.
- Select which exhibits she wants to see.

What other basic features do you think this app must have? Do you think it's essential that a user of this application be able to search for a specific type of sea creature to find where it's located, or is that just nice-to-have?

Performance and Delight Features

In addition to basic features, consider *performance* and *delight* features. Designers sometimes use Kano Analysis to break these features out into groups: http://uxmag.com/articles/leveraging-the-kano-model-for-optimal-results

PERFORMANCE

Performance features are often competitive with features from other solutions. People are more satisfied when your solution has them, and dissatisfied when it doesn't (but they'll weigh their dissatisfaction against their satisfaction with other features you offer).

Take our airline example. Performance features of an airline trip could be extra leg room. If another airline has less leg room but offers free gourmet snacks and headphones for watching movies, a traveler will weigh the competitive performance features against each other when making his choice.

DELIGHT

Delight features are those that are unexpected - perhaps no other competitors have them - and they add a sense of fun, surprise, or meaning to your solution. For example, on overnight flights, British Airways gives passengers a "comfort" kit with sleeping mask, socks, toothbrush and toothpaste.

People don't expect a delight feature, so they aren't dissatisfied if it's not in your solution. But having a delight feature can lead to greater user satisfaction. When your solution's users are delighted, they're more likely to use the solution again - and more likely to tell others about it.

Activity:
Splattering Features

 45 Minutes   1 + Player

Pretend it's your job to create a mobile application for the Nemo Aquarium (p. 90). Hold a mini-brainstorm session to think up app features that fulfill basic user requirements, meet users' performance feature expectations, and add a few extras to surprise and delight them. Write descriptions or sketch simple icons of your features below:

Basic Features	Performance Features	Delight Features
		FISH BUBBLE GAME

Under Prioritization Pressure

Just as you had to cut away concepts at the beginning of this chapter, you'll probably also feel some pressure to cut away some of the features on your list.

You can start by using the same factors we covered when evaluating concepts for the Nemo Aquarium (p. 93), such as context of use, design principles, and feasibility.

You may still have too many features, but you won't know for sure until you develop more detailed visual or interactive designs for your concept, using techniques such as sketching or prototyping.

Expressing your designs visually brings out the features that are causing pressure - crowding the areas where users can see and interact with your solution (the interface), or blocking access to important features.

Pressure isn't a bad thing. It helps you categorize your basic, performance, and delight features. Also, pressure helps you and your team give up features that seem exciting or interesting, but don't really contribute to the impact of the solution.

Put yourself under prioritization pressure by sketching a better backpack in the activity on the next page.

Considering a Feature...

Does it directly and uniquely solve a problem that you know is important for your target users?

If it's removed, is it unlikely your solution will solve important problems (or unlikely that people will use it)?

Does it fit the context of use? (p. 86)

Does it follow your design principles? (p. 84)

Is it feasible and viable? (p. 88)

Is it a key performance feature? Or, does it add an aspect of delight (meaning, surprise, or fun) without detracting from important basic or performance features? (p. 95)

Activity:
Back That Pack Up: Prioritize Your Features

 45 Minutes   1+ Player

Why would you include some features and not others? Learn about the need for feature prioritization in this sketch activity. Decorate the three blank backpacks below with features from the list on the right (or other features that you dream up on your own!). Follow the instructions regarding how many features to sketch directly onto each backpack.

- **Basic:** One compartment with a zipper and straps
- **Performance:** Phone pocket, headphone clip, drink bottle clip, belt strap, padded straps, water resistant
- **Delight:** Solar panels, yoga mat carrier, inflatable pillow, attached bedroll, collapsible bag poncho

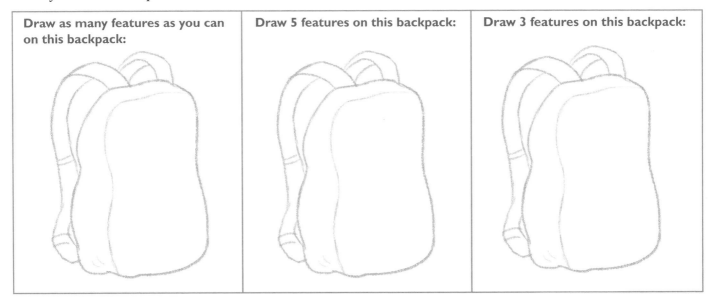

Draw as many features as you can on this backpack:

Draw 5 features on this backpack:

Draw 3 features on this backpack:

Interactive Prototypes

Even after you've sketched, your chosen features may not be in complete harmony. You won't know for sure until you create a variation on your concept that demonstrates how a person may use it. A *prototype* is an expression of your solution that lets you or a potential user mimic interacting with it.

- Prototypes can range from low-fidelity (such as a series of sketches) to high-fidelity (such as a fully working version of a physical product or digital app).

You sketched a low-fidelity version of a backpack. If you actually sew together a model backpack that someone could wear, you've made a higher-fidelity prototype.

Why create a prototype?

- Prototypes make your solution more real to your team. You'll get a better feeling for how people will interact with it, and a shared team understanding when discussing which features to include and which to cut.

- You'll begin to see how features interact with each other - which features are stronger when combined with others, and which seem disconnected.

- You'll have something you can test with potential users - which you're well on the way to doing in this chapter.

Digital solutions tend to be easier to express and test with a sketched prototype. Let's sketch one and test it out! We'll use the case of TooCooks.

TooCooks

Too often cooking can be the lonely job of an individual. Sometimes it seems as if kitchens work only for one person - or for two people who cook together often. But cooking can be educational, fun, and collaborative. It can bring together people who may not know each other well, or those looking for a new activity.

TooCooks is a solution that makes cooking with another person easier and more fun by assessing skill levels and assigning steps accordingly. Each recipe step is timed, and waiting periods are filled with interactive challenges like conversation starters or trivia questions.

CONSTRAINTS

- Design for only two cooks at a time of potentially different ages and skill levels. For example, cooks can be an adult and a child, or two adults on a date.
- Design for one shared device during the cooking.

DESIGN PRINCIPLES

- Those with lower skill levels should feel like an important, valuable member of the team.
- Playful interaction wins over culinary perfection.
- Celebrate the kitchen as the heart of the home.

FEATURES

- A *cook profile* that stores information about a player's skill level, food preferences, and allergies. This should be gathered via a short questionnaire and stored for use during multiple cooking events.
- A *kitchen profile* to determine what kinds of equipment or utensils will generally be available.
- An *event picker* that allows players to choose the tone of the cooking event (such as "Romantic," "Educational," "Silly"), the meal type (breakfast, lunch, dinner), and how many people are dining.
- *Recipe suggestions* (three to six) based on data from the event picker, the kitchen profile, and cook profiles, with a way for players to choose one of the recipes.
- A *recipe stepper* for the chosen recipe, with timed tasks and audible alerts customized for each cook playing.
- A *fun gap-filler!* Consider conversation starters, mini-games, trivia, or educational challenges. These will appear while players are waiting for water to boil. Players should be able to pause and resume.

TooCooks: Personas

LONG-TERM LAWSON

Personal Information

Age: 25 years old

Lawson moved to Chicago for work about a year ago. He's at a point in his life where he's looking for a serious relationship. He's excited about Jessica - they've been on several dates together, and for this one he wants to plan something more interesting than a restaurant and a movie.

Goals

- Have a fun date that helps the two of them get to know each other better.
- Impress Jessica with his home, and with his desire to develop a serious relationship.

Frustrations

- So many recipe sites call for ingredients or utensils that he doesn't have yet! He doesn't want to buy half his kitchen.
- Lawson doesn't know if Jessica is a great cook or a pure beginner. An overcomplicated recipe could backfire. He wants to look open and fun, but not ridiculous.

MAKE-A-HOME MEGAN

Personal Information

Age: 36 years old

Megan recently married Ben, who has a 10-year-old daughter named Angie. Megan wants to get to know Angie in a way that's friendly and home-oriented. She'd like to be an important and positive person in Angie's life.

Goals

- Strengthen her relationship with Angie.
- Form traditions for their new home together.

Frustrations

- Most nights Megan, Angie, and Ben end up in front of the television. It's easy but impersonal. Megan wants an interesting way to spend one-on-one time with Angie doing something active that they'll both enjoy.
- Angie hasn't done much cooking, and she can get anxious when faced with a challenge that she doesn't understand. Megan doesn't want Angie to get stressed out over making something perfect. She just wants them both to have a good time creating something together.

Sketching a Digital Prototype

When you're working with digital solutions, you don't have to show all of your features and their interactive elements (such as buttons and fields) at once. You can make some elements appear or hide based on what the user does. Or, you can spread elements across multiple screens that users access one by one. That allows you to fit more features into a product.

Take a look at the following interface elements. They're part of a questionnaire, which will generate the cook profile feature mentioned on page 100. Here, they're scattered around on one page. Using the mobile phone outlines you'll find next, sketch in these elements over three screens. If you feel a particular element is unnecessary based on your priorities, drop it!

Activity:
Sketch for a Cook

Use the design challenge on page 100 and the elements on page 102 to sketch a three-screen prototype.

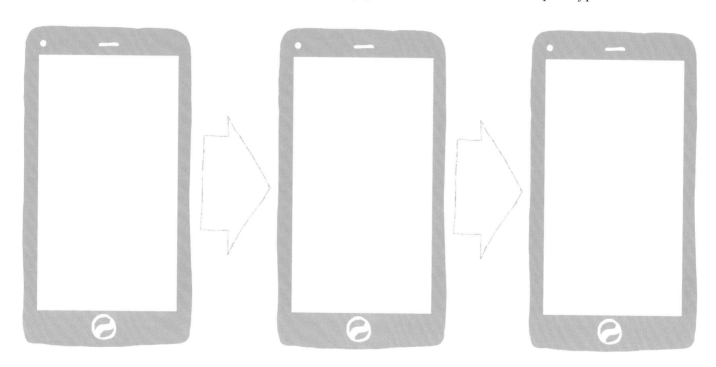

Hey you down here: if you were designing a real mobile interface, users would also be able to scroll down to see more features. But we're keeping this example simple, so try keeping all features on one screen and assume there's no scrolling. Stumped? See how we did it on page 145.

Testing a Paper Prototype

Finished with your sketching? You just created a prototype! Those three screens represent steps of a particular task a user should be able to complete within the TooCooks solution. But how easily could they complete it? Would the person you're designing for know how to interact with your prototype, and what impact would their interactions have?

Let's finish up a prototype and find out. It's time to choose your own adventure. You can:

1 Add two to four screens of your own sketches and test them with someone else. This is a good option if you're working solo, although you'll need to find a few friendly folks to test what you come up with.

2 Level up and take on one of the other features from TooCooks on page 100 from scratch, like the event picker, or recipe stepper. If you're working in a larger group, individuals or small teams can each take a different feature to prototype, then test the results across teams.

How to Do It:

- Copy or print multiple pages of the templates on the next page, and use them to sketch your screens.
- Cut out each screen to make individual pages.
- Place the first screen in front of someone who will test the prototype. Ideally, it's someone who fits your target user group; but for this activity, don't let it stop you if someone else is willing!
- Ask a few initial questions (like those on the next page). Then ask your test participant to complete a particular task.
- When she says she would select something that would take her to another screen (have her point it out on the page), remove the page she's looking at and replace it with the new one. If you don't have a page for a particular screen, just tell her that screen hasn't been designed yet.
- Repeat until your test participant gets confused and gives up, or finishes the task.
- Repeat with other people. Try for five!

Run a test yourself, using the following activity sheets. Remember your skills from Sponge: avoid leading questions, and don't give participants the answers too quickly. Listen to them!

Templates for Test Screens

Copy or print these to sketch screens. You can also find free templates online: http://www.interfacesketch.com/

Test Questions

Write your test questions, keeping in mind some of the skills you developed in Sponge. You can revisit them on pages 10, 13, and 16.

If you're not sure which questions to ask, try these:

- Look at the first screen. What do you think this is? What might you use it for?
- Show me how you would [complete this quiz]. (Note, replace that task with whichever task you're testing.)
- Share your impressions of that task. Was it easier or more difficult than you thought it would be?
- What could be made more clear?
- How could it be improved?
- What did you like? Dislike?

Testing Activity

Test Questions:

_____

_____

_____

_____

_____

Participant Info:

Name: _____ Age: _____

Relevant info such as occupation: _____

Answers and observations from this test:

Interesting quotes, areas of confusion, likes or dislikes...

_____

_____

_____

106

After the Test

You just finished a usability test! If you were working as a professional researcher, there would be quite a bit more to it. But as informal as this test was, it can still tell you a great deal and save design heartache later.

Be careful when analyzing your results. Try to keep that objective researcher's eye when you're considering the impact of issues or suggestions that came up.

Analysis is one of the most difficult parts of conducting research!

What makes analysis hard? After all, you have direct feedback. The next steps should be clear, right?

Well, on one hand, you don't want to dismiss someone's feedback just because it doesn't support a favorite feature or element that you'd like to include. Ideally, you test several people (5-10) so that it's clear when something is really an issue.

On the other hand, you don't want to react to every comment, and change your design completely, every time you talk to a new person!

Analysis involves a difficult yet important aspect of a designer's job: to take in a lot of information, such as context of use, design principles, and now direct user feedback, and weigh them all to make decisions.

These decisions could be:

- Which problems to solve
- Which Solution Ideas to sketch as concepts
- Which concepts to use when refining details
- Which tasks to test
- Which features to include
- How to design elements expressing those features
- How to incorporate feedback affecting all of the above

And guess what? You've done most of this already! Be sure to do the last one, too. Take the feedback from your test, and revise your screens in a way that you think improves your solution.

Game:
Improv Testing: Prototype Theater

Goal
Take your prototyping skills to the next level with this real-time testing game that turns your paper prototype into an interactive puppet show.

What You'll Need
- Colored markers, pens, or pencils
- 2 poster boards
- Large sheets of paper (about 11 by 17 inches)
- 2 pairs of scissors

Step 1: Divide and Design
Separate into two groups. Each group is going to design a paper prototype for the same Challenge statement, then act as the test subjects for each other's solutions.

Step 2: Pick a Digital Challenge Statement
Pick a Challenge statement! You can use one from this chapter; one you've been working on for each final challenge; or make up a new one. **Your Challenge statement must require the teams to design a mobile digital solution, such as an app or mobile website.**

Step 3: From Poster Board to Handheld Device
Draw on and cut your poster board to make it resemble an oversized mobile device. Consider the screen shape and don't forget to include physical elements, such as buttons. Cut out the screen so that the poster is a frame.

Step 4: Create your Solution Elements
Spend time with your group designing your solution. Consider which features you plan to create, and think through the user interactions from start to finish. Once you have a solid plan, sketch the screens and screen elements. Where possible, draw screen elements that will change – such as icons or buttons – on a separate sheet of paper, and cut them out so they can "move" around on your screen.

Step 5: Testing, Testing!
Coordinate your team so that one person is holding up your "device" frame. Have other team members hold up the paper pieces of your team's solution in the screen space. As the testers interact with the screen elements, have the puppeteers react by re-arranging the paper pieces "on screen." Try to improvise multiple user paths based on testers' feedback. Try guiding users through two different interaction sequences, and ask testers which they liked better.

Physical Prototypes: Totally Doable

Making a physical prototype may sound expensive, difficult, and time-consuming; but a ton of cost-effective resources are out there to help you bring your design into the real world, or the digital space.

At any craft store, you can purchase clay, foam core, and other physical components to create working models of your design. Some clays, such as Sculpey or plaster, can be baked or set to harden, creating solid and durable physical models of your own creation! Don't be afraid to borrow from or otherwise alter existing objects, too. You can find almost anything at second-hand stores for cheap, so you can experiment with taking objects apart and reconfiguring them according to your own design. A little paint can hide just about any unsightly physical hacking.

In the digital space, tools such as Axure or Balsamiq allow you to create animated, digital "wireframe" prototypes that you can easily alter after testing. Websites like Code.org offer free tutorials and other resources that can set you on the path to becoming your own developer. Downloading a free trial of software that you want to learn, or taking a class via Lynda.com, can help expand your skills. Some 3D printing companies, like Shapeways, enable you to submit your own designs, which they will print and send back to you.

The Maker Movement

The Maker Movement, also known as DIY (Do It Yourself) culture, is a growing global trend in which people design and self-manufacture useful or entertaining objects at home using a mix of traditional and digital tools. A number of maker subculture websites feature tutorials, message boards with oodles of advice, and other reference resources. Among them are:

Noisebridge
www.noisebridge.net

Pumping Station: One
www.pumpingstationone.org

MAKE magazine
www.makezine.com

This site offers content, but also reports on developments in the maker community, including the annual Maker Faire, which attracts tens of thousands of people worldwide.

THE SCULPT CHALLENGE!

You've come a long way from your first Sponge challenge. Now it's time to test and refine your Solution Idea to see how it may play in the real world!

Prototype your concept and test it with four to five people.

If you've been developing the same Solution Idea into concepts throughout this book, you can continue to use that concept here.

If you'd like to take on this Challenge using concepts based on a different Solution Idea, you could also use one of the cases in this book to generate concepts (using techniques from Splatter) and refine them into a prototype for testing.

"Sleepin' with the Fishes, Sea?" (pp 90-92) and "TooCooks" (pp 100-101) both include digital Solution Ideas you could work from. They may also provide a good avenue if your original concept is physical and you're not sure how to prototype it.

If you choose to work through this book more than once, you can try each one!

Testing Activity

Test Questions:

_____

_____

_____

_____

_____

Participant info:

Name: _____ **Age:** _____

**Relevant info
like occupation:** _____

Answers and observations from this test:

Interesting quotes, areas of confusion, likes or dislikes...

_____

_____

_____

_____

Spark Summary

We propose this solution:

_____

_____

To achieve these results:

_____

_____

Our overall challenge is to:

_____

_____

**We know of these
problems:**

_____

_____

For a full SPARK statement, see
the example on page 30 or use
the template on page 50.

Challenges You Can Chew

Details on design principles

"Creating Great Design Principles: 6 Counter-intuitive Tests" by Jared Spool

http://www.uie.com/articles/creating-design-principles

A Project Guide to UX Design, Second Edition by Unger and Chandler (New Riders, 2012). Chapter 10: Design Principles, and Chapter 13: Prototyping

Useful for usability testing

Rocket Surgery Made Easy by Steve Krug (New Riders, 2009)

The Debrief

That was it. Right there. That was the moment. If you're reading this, you've just finished one iteration of the process that Experience Designers go through when creating a concept for something brand spanking new. (Or you've skipped ahead from previous chapters, Spoilers!)

"Just one iteration," you ask? Yes, it's true. A designer may go through many iterations with her work. She may try a path, test and refine it, and work through that path again. When she's gone through Sculpt, the feedback she hears may lead her to reframe her Spark question and repeat Splatter. Then back through Sculpt!

It's ok to iterate. It's not a failure when you learn and adjust. After all, you probably gathered some feedback in your testing that led you to refine. It's better to incorporate that feedback now, rather than when you try to develop something into a real solution and potentially waste money and time in the process!

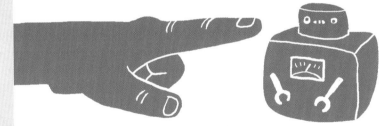

You may have heard this question: "If a tree falls in the forest and no one is there to hear it, does it make a sound?" Well, if a designer creates a concept, but doesn't make an effort to explain why it's important, it probably doesn't make much of an impact. In the last step, Storytell, you'll learn how to represent your creation in a way that matters to those who may use it - or help you build it!

Storytell!

You're About to:

Get branded *

Write your own bible

Give an elevator pitch

Get a crash course in marketing **

* Don't worry, no hot irons are involved!
** Good thing we've been designing helmets!!

Did You Know?

Storytelling predates the written word. Humans passed spoken-word stories from person to person until we developed the ability to communicate with letters, numbers, and pictures.

Some storytelling conventions resonate through the ages. Variations on the opening phrase, "Once upon a time," have appeared in literature since 1380. The equallyubiquitous closing line, "Happily ever after," has been around just as long, but it didn't always sound so cheerful. Children's fairytales pre-1600 often featured the ending, "Happily until their deaths." Doesn't exactly have the same pep, does it?

Storytelling is the most basic form of human communication. We use stories to express our needs and feelings to each other. We build relationships by sharing stories. We tell stories to educate, challenge, entertain, and inform each other. We even think in stories. When you wake up in the morning and think, "I'm going to design a music game today," you are telling yourself the best story of all... your own! Designers storytell to communicate the value of their solutions.

The ways we storytell are constantly changing, but some stories continue to delight us, even thousands of years later. Visitors still flock to see the Paleolithic era cave paintings in Lascaux, France, that our ancient ancestors painted more than 17,000 years ago. Historians and amateur enthusiasts alike still peruse the millions of pictograms known as hieroglyphics that the ancient Egyptians carved into stone walls and pressed into clay tablets about 5,000 years ago. And thanks to Johannes Gutenberg's invention, the printing press, the famed plays and sonnets of Shakespeare have never gone out of print.

Today, we still create sequential picture stories and write books, but we have countless new ways to storytell, too. From augmented reality mobile apps to video games, contemporary storytelling is more immersive than ever.

As designers, we need to be strategic storytellers. You need to pick the most effective and engaging way to tell the story of your solution. You not only have to keep in mind what that story is, but how you tell it, who you are telling it to, and even when and where your audience will experience it. A highway billboard that drivers glance at might not be the best place to tell the story of your cat sign language system.

The rewards of successful storytelling are great: Your audience will not only utilize your solution, but also share the story of your solution with others, encouraging them to use it, too. Now that's a happy ending!

Throughout **SPONGE**, **SPARK**, **SPLATTER**, and **SCULPT**, you've focused on the design process: Developing a solution that answers a need or improves a condition, and through a series of exercises, expanding and refining it. In **STORYTELL**, you will stop developing the solution itself, and instead focus on presenting your solution to the people for whom you designed it. After all, if they don't know that your solution exists, people will never use it.

Why did you buy the shoes you're wearing, and not another pair? Why did you choose to install certain apps on your mobile device and not others? Chances are that good solution storytelling influenced your decision. You picked those solutions because you liked their personalities. Branding is the process of bringing personality to your solution. The art of sharing that story with other people is called marketing. Together, these skillsets enable you to effectively **STORYTELL**, informing and engaging an audience with your solution.

Questions to Ponder:
- If your solution were a person, what would he or she look like?
- Why do people use one solution instead of another?
- How do you compel people to use your solution?

What You'll Do:
- Develop a personality for your solution
- Construct the building blocks for effective storytelling
- Get comfortable sharing that story with an audience

Storytelling Challenges

There are many challenges your storytelling must overcome to connect your solution with your audience:

- Attention: From TV commercials to ads on the bus, there are solution stories everywhere! You need to entice your audience to focus on your story.
- Budget: Not every storyteller can afford a Super Bowl commercial. You need to be a strategic storyteller, engaging with your audience when and where your story will get the most valuable exposure.
- Time: Your storytelling needs to to convince your audience that it's worth their time to change their habits or thinking to utilize your solution.

Brands Are Solutions... with Personality

The terms "brand" and "branding" come from the days of cowboys, when ranchers used to burn unique, personalized symbols into the hides of their cattle so they could tell who owned which ones. Ouch!

Today, "branding" is a process that is used to develop the uniqueness of your solution. A brand can be a company, a physical object, a service or process, a digital application or software - even a person! Brands distinguish solutions from one another.

You encounter hundreds of brands every day. For example, if you want a cup of coffee, you might choose between buying some from Starbucks, Dunkin' Donuts, or a locally owned cafe. Which would you pick? Each of these coffees has a unique brand, but they are all the same solution: the tasty beverage, coffee! Why did you pick one brand instead of the others? Your purchase decision was likely influenced by a preference for the "personality" of your brand of choice.

Some brands have been around for so long, and their storytelling has been so successful, that people commonly use the brand name instead of the solution name. For example, if you have a stuffy nose, what do you blow your nose in? Chances are, you said "Kleenex," instead of "facial tissue." Kleenex is a brand. Facial tissue is a solution. There are many facial tissue brands, but only one Kleenex. A company called Kimberly-Clark first started selling Kleenex in the United States in 1924.

Can you think of some other brand names that are commonly used in the place of solution names?

Activity:
Name That Brand

 10-15 Minutes  1 Player

Try to guess the brand name of the solution, based on the hints below. (Answers on page 146.)

If you get a boo-boo or a scrape, you might put one of these adhesive wound coverings over it:

_____

You might tread through this fake green grass on a professional football field:

_____

Kids love to "pop" the air-filled plastic pockets on this packaging material, which is often used to protect fragile objects during travel:

_____

This toy disc glides through the air horizontally. You might play catch with it at the park:

_____

Regardless of the search engine you are using, this brand name is often used when you are searching a term or phrase on the Internet:

_____

This popular table-top game is a lot like tennis, but it uses paddles and much smaller, lighter balls:

_____

You've probably written yourself a reminder on these little yellow notes, which have an adhesive strip on their back:

_____

You clean your ears with these cotton-tipped swab sticks:

_____

Game:
Brand-y Land

118

Goal
You are probably already familiar with more branding than you think. Find out which team has a black belt in branding with this guessing game.

What You'll Need
- Pen & paper
- A large bowl
- Timer or stopwatch

Step 1: Ladies & Gentlemen, Pick Your Brands!
Divide the paper up evenly so that everyone has five slips of paper. Without talking to one another, everyone must write down one brand on each of their pieces of paper. Fold each piece of paper twice, and put them all in the same, large bowl. (And hang on to these strips of paper! You can re-use them in the Game on page 127.)

Step 2: Team Up
Divide into even teams, and flip a coin to see which team goes first.

Step 3: Brandtastic!
The team that gets to go first should unanimously select one player to start. That player should stand up where everyone can see her, and have the bowl easily within reach. The other team sets the timer for 60 seconds. During that minute, the player from the active team will grab slips of paper from the bowl, one at a time. She must try to describe the brand on the paper without using the brand name while her teammates try to guess the brand. If the team guesses correctly, she keeps that slip of paper. If she accidentally says the brand name, then the slip of paper gets folded back up and put back into the bowl. If the team gets stuck on a clue, she may fold the clue back up, put it back in the bowl, and select another. Don't reveal the brands that the team cannot guess!

Step 4: Scoring
When the minute is up, count up how many slips of paper the team was able to guess correctly. That is the team's score for Round 1. Do not put those slips back in the bowl.

Step 5: Finishing
Repeat Step 3, alternating which team is guessing and rotating the player giving clues, until no slips of paper are left. The team with the most slips of paper at the end wins!

Brand Building Blocks: Show Some Promise

The foundation of branding is the Brand Promise. The *Brand Promise* is a statement that sums up the need your solution promises to fulfill, or the improvement it promises to deliver. For example, "Dracula SunShield prevents vampires from catching fire when exposed to sunlight." The Brand Promise is an important focusing statement for all of your storytelling efforts, and helps you succinctly explain to your audience what a solution does. Does this sound familiar? It should! The Brand Promise is akin to your Challenge statement:

CHALLENGE STATEMENT		
Make this activity...	improved in this way (more, less...)	for these people:
Going out during the daytime	*less painful*	*vampires*

BRAND PROMISE		
This solution (name it)...	offers this fix or improvement	for these people:
Dracula SunShield	*prevents skin from catching fire in sunlight*	*vampires who want to go out during the day*

How is the Brand Promise different from the Challenge statement? Check it out:

Challenge Statement

- Call to action expressing an unsolved need, problem, or opportunity for improvement
- Aimed at designers
- No solution exists yet, so you have no story to tell

Brand Promise

- Declarative statement communicating a solution that fixes a problem or improves a condition
- Aimed at a particular user audience
- You have a story to tell that explains how the solution works
- Fun! The solution has a name!

Activity:
Pinky Swear: Make a (Brand) Promise

 20 Minutes    1 + Player

Try your hand at transforming a Challenge statement into a Brand Promise. What brands do you know and use that fulfill these Challenge statement? Fill in the Brand Promise for those branded solutions.

CHALLENGE STATEMENT		
Make this activity...	**improved in this way (more, less...)**	**for these people:**
Recognizing a song you hear in public	Easier	music lovers

BRAND PROMISE		
This solution...	**offers this fix or improvement**	**for these people:**
Hint: It's an app...		

CHALLENGE STATEMENT		
Make this activity...	**improved in this way (more, less...)**	**for these people:**
Watching long movies	More comfortable	Thirsty movie goers

BRAND PROMISE		
This solution...	**offers this fix or improvement**	**for these people:**
Hint: You read about it in this book...		

Stacking Brand Building Blocks: Truth & the Universe

Underlying every Brand Promise is a Universal Truth. The *Universal Truth* is not specific to your solution. It expresses the human (or nonhuman in the case of Dracula SunShield) motivation for the need, or the desire for the improvement in your Brand Promise.

The Universal Truth is key to helping you communicate why someone would want to use your solution. This should sound familiar, too! The Universal Truth builds upon your Spark:

SPARK	
Considering these problems...	**we'll spark solution ideas by asking:**
- *Flammable vampire skin* - *12 hours of daylight*	*How might we use existing skin care methods to protect vampires?*

Your solution may have many Universal Truths. During the branding process, you must select one Universal Truth to focus your story. How might each of the

different Universal Truths for Dracula SunShield (below) affect the way you'd tell the story of that solution? Can you think of a third Universal Truth? Write it in below:

UNIVERSAL TRUTH	
Considering these problems...	**We'll share these enticing messages:**
1 – *Flammable vampire skin*	1 – *Flaming skin hurts! Avoid painful burns*
2 – *12 hours of daylight*	2 – *Don't miss out on daytime activities!*
3 –	3 –

The Brand Speaks! Voice & Tone

What were some of the words and phrases you called out during the Brand-y Land game? These nouns and adjectives express how the brand makes you feel, or describes how you feel about the solution. These feelings and descriptions are known as Brand Voice and Tone.

VOICE

Brand Voice is literally *how* you speak when you are speaking as your brand. It is the personality expressed by the accent, choice of words, and other easily recognizable qualities of your communication. To define Brand Voice, imagine that your brand is a person. What would it look and sound like? Would it be male or female? Would it use lots of slang or speak formally? Try to craft a Brand Voice based on characteristics that you are familiar with, otherwise you run the risk of crafting a Voice that seems fake, or worse, insulting. Here is the same story in two different Voices:

Missed the boat on sleep? Mermaid Song Tea is your ticket to slumberland.

ArrRRR! Crankier than a sleepy sailor?! Let Mermaid Song Tea luuuure you to sweet dreams.

TONE

Brand Tone motivates you to say what you do when you are speaking as your brand. It is your brand's perspective on life, expressed by the mood and message of your communication. Defining Brand Tone is like creating a psychological profile for your brand. Is your brand an optimist, or a pessimist? Think of qualities that you admire in people you know, and use those as inspiration when producing your Brand Tone. Here is the same story in two different Tones:

Don't fight the siren's song. Embrace your dreams: Mermaid Song Tea.

Healthy, deep sleep is not a myth. Drink Mermaid Song Tea.

Activity:
Picturing Brand Persona: Voice vs. Tone

Another way to consider the difference between Voice and Tone is to visualize your solution as if it were a person (or animal or supernatural creature). Voice is all the superficial qualities of your brand. What would someone learn about your brand if they just looked at it? Draw these Voice characteristics of your brand (or one of your choosing) below. For example, if your brand is a female princess, draw a dress and add a crown. Tone is the "internal" quality of your brand. Is your brand happy or sad? Optimistic or pessimistic? Energetic or lethargic? Write these words inside the outline of your brand.

Activity:
Brand Voice Karaoke: Tweet Re-Mix

 30 Minutes 1+ Player

Imagine that you are the brand manager for a popular fast food chain that is about to use Twitter to announce the addition of a new burger to its menu. Exercise your skills by re-writing each Tweet in a different brand voice:

Original Tweet = Generic burger chain voice:

"Our new mini-burgers are so delicious, you won't be able to eat just one!"

A haughty, designer burger chain for busy runway models:

"Oooh, la-la. Our scrumptious mini-burgers are so 'in,' dahlink, you'll eat your dress size!"

A high-seas, adventure-themed burger chain for little boys who want to be pirates:

_____

A family burger chain that features a play place for kids and a quiet sit-down area for busy parents:

_____

The first burger chain to welcome cat owners to eat alongside their pets:

_____

A Viking-themed burger chain for loud people who often enter eating competitions:

_____

A burger chain focused on elderly, penny-pinching retirees who like to eat alone:

_____

An island-themed burger chain that compares eating its food to taking a relaxing, tropical vacation:

_____

An exciting circus-themed restaurant where live stunts are performed for patrons while they eat:

_____

An all-year-round Halloween-themed burger place that's a popular date place for teenagers:

_____

Keep Your Story Straight: Brand Bibles

As a solution becomes more successful, the ability to maintain a cohesive brand presence can be incredibly difficult. Think of a brand like Coca-Cola, which has been in existence since 1892 - more than 120 years! On any given day, hundreds of Coca-Cola employees make decisions that represent the brand: choosing the words for a packaging label, selecting music to play in a TV commercial, deciding what to post on the company's Facebook page. How do they keep all their communication "on-brand," or consistent with one master brand identity?

Easy. They have a bible. A brand bible.

Brand bibles are reference documents detailing all the elements of a brand's identity. Centralizing this information helps keep all brand storytelling aligned with the Brand Promise, Universal Truth, and Voice and Tone, among other elements.

The brand bible is a living document, which means that it can grow and change over time.

Besides the Brand Promise, Universal Truth, and Voice and Tone, a bible can contain storytelling elements such as:

- Visual design elements, such as logos, illustrations of mascots or other characters, particular color hues, fonts, and other graphics
- Text such as catchphrases, taglines, official solution descriptions, and directions
- Solution photography and/or images of people interacting with the solution
- Special music, sound effects, jingles, or other auditory trademarks
- Videos and animations

Brand Meets World: Make Your Marketing

Now that you have established your solution's brand, it's time to explore how to share that story with your audience. The strategy of how, where, when, and to whom you tell your brand story is called marketing.

Marketing is not passive storytelling. Effective marketing is storytelling with a goal known as the "call to action." If your marketing is successful, it will compel your audience to respond to your call to action. Broadly, these audience reactions fall into three categories:

- Using the solution
- Buying the solution
- Telling other people about the solution

It is very challenging to successfully convince a user to respond to your call to action because innumerable other brands are competing for his time, attention, and money.

No two marketing efforts are alike, but most successful marketing stories do two things very well:

- They communicate the solution value quickly and clearly. (This is where your brand bible can help!)

- They storytell in a unique and engaging manner.

While branding needs to be consistent to build familiarity and trust with your audience, marketing needs change and updating to entertain your audience. Even if your solution story is a good one, no one wants to hear the same story, told the same way, over and over again!

Game:
Going Up? Elevator Pitch

Goal

Think you have simple brand storytelling mastered? Be the first player to pitch your way to the top of the top of the game board. A "pitch" is a very short - usually one or two sentence - marketing story.

What You'll Need

- A timer or stopwatch
- The slips of paper with brand names (and the bowl) from the Brand-y Land Game on page 118. If you haven't played this game yet, complete Step 1 of Brand-y Land to create them.

Step 1: Pitchers & Catchers

Select one player to be the catcher. The rest of the players are pitchers. Seat yourselves so that the pitchers are sitting next to each other, opposite the catcher, with a wide table or floor space between you.

Step 2: Build the Game Board

Randomly select slips of paper from the bowl and place them face down on the table between the pitchers and the catcher... without looking at them! Arrange one column of paper slips in front of each pitcher. As long as all the columns are the same length, they can be as long as you want. Make them at least five rows deep.

Step 3: Batter Up!

Have the catcher pick a number between 1 and 10. The first pitcher to guess that number, or come the closest to it, goes first.

Step 4: Step into the Elevator

Have the catcher start the timer. Once the clock starts, the pitcher can turn over one slip of paper in any column, but it must be in the first row (the row closest to the pitchers). The pitcher has 10 seconds to give the catcher a sales pitch on that solution. At the end of the 10 seconds, the catcher must give a thumbs up (I'd buy it) or a thumbs down (Not worth my time). If the catcher gives a thumbs up, that same pitcher gets to write their initials on that slip of paper. Then, they get to go again, this time flipping over any slip from the second row. If the pitcher got a thumbs down, then the next pitcher is up (going clockwise) and must pick a slip of paper from the first row. The new pitcher can either choose the already turned-over brand, or turn over a new one.

Step 5: Pitch Your Way to the Top

Keep repeating Step 4 until one pitcher wins by being the first to pitch their way across the game board, adding their initials to one slip of paper in every row.

Audience Dictionary

The following terms can be used interchangeably to refer to the audience for a solution, but each one has a slightly different meaning.

User - Typically used to refer to a digital audience

Consumer - Usually refers to the audience for a physical solution that might be purchased, used up, and then purchased again

Customer - Oftentimes means the audience who has to pay for the solution

You Talkin' to Me? Know Your Audience

In the Elevator Pitch game, what tactics did the winning player employ to get to the top? What did he or she say? Chances are, it was not only *what* he or she said, but how the comments targeted that specific catcher who was the audience for your marketing storytelling pitches.

Knowing your audience enables you to position your marketing so that it makes the most sense to them, such as how to present the benefits of the Brand Promise and the Universal Truth, or what features to emphasize. For example, how differently would you market the same pair of jogging sneakers to someone who you know is dieting compared to someone who is a running enthusiast?

Your audience may or may not be the same person for whom you designed your solution. For example, if you created singing diapers that help toddlers pottytrain, the consumers of the solution are tots. But the customer, who is actually purchasing your solution, is the parent.

Even if your audience is the same as your user - say, bald bikers - you will now need to think of them in different terms than when you were designing a solution for them. When you were crafting a solution, you had to consider their needs and wants in the context of using your solution. But when you are marketing to them, you have to consider under what conditions they make purchasing decisions, or what motivates them to respond to your call to action.

Smooth Operator: The Art of Marketing

Now that you're a rockstar at communicating your purpose quickly and clearly, it's time to talk about how to make your story entertaining. Successful marketing keeps your message intact, but adds to it:

- Novelty
- Entertainment
- Personalization

These are not rules. Think of the them as starting points for brainstorming a good way to tell your solution story. Let's dig a little deeper into those starting points.

Novelty in marketing means that your story is in some way unique. People tend to pay special attention to things they have never seen before, or things they are not accustomed to (or are forbidden from) seeing. Many marketing stories leverage new technologies or social taboos to remain fresh. You can tap into your solution's novelty by considering your brand persona. Can your persona do something that your audience cannot?

Entertainment in marketing means that your story engages your audience's emotions. Whether they are laughing or crying, when people experience an emotion in connection with a brand story, they form a bond with it. Think about the emotions your audience might feel when they are using your solution, or as a result of using it. Can you find a way to make them feel that emotion with your storytelling before they try your solution?

Personalization in marketing means that your story feels customized to each of your audience members. People enjoy feeling special, like they are not part of the crowd. People also tend to pay more attention when a story directly includes them or if they are invested in it. Letting your audience incorporate their own photos, words, or ideas in your solution story (like a contest!) builds that bond.

You can't guarantee that people will laugh at a joke you tell at a party, and you can't create a sure-fire formula for a successful marketing story. But these guidelines can help you on your way!

Case Study Comparison: Livin' on the Edge

Oftentimes, marketers will cleverly leverage social taboos to tell a solution story that grabs attention and drives conversation. Audiences, however, are unpredictable. You never know how a controversial topic will be perceived. Let's look at two examples that had very opposite public reactions:

Company Name: Kmart

Solution being marketed: Free shipping for members of Kmart's Shop Your Way program, when the product they want isn't available in store.

Marketing: In a 36-second YouTube video, a variety of different shoppers exclaim in a Kmart store, "I shipped my pants!" or "I shipped my drawers!" If said aloud quickly, these phrases make the word "shipped" sound like a four-letter word that is not generally used in mainstream marketing.

Results: 13 million unique YouTube views in one week, plus countless news reports, social media conversations, and other posts of the video across the Internet. Despite some public condemnations from social advocacy groups (such as One Million Moms), the video continues to gain views, advertising awards, and press. Kmart even produced a follow-up YouTube video featuring another cheeky play on words one month later.

Company Name: Hyundai

Solution being marketed: The Hyundai ix35 fuel cell car, which emits harmless water vapor instead of poisonous carbon dioxide.

Marketing: In a one-minute online video targeting the UK market, a man attempts to commit suicide by running a pipe from his car's tailpipe into the sealed Hyundai ix35. However, the man is unable to kill himself because unlike other automobiles, the car's emissions are harmless.

Result: A viewer who had lost her father to this form of suicide wrote a blog post condemning the commercial. The blog post and Hyundai video were posted together on YouTube, and went viral. The exact number of views is unknown because Hyundai tried to remove the video, but it was posted and shared faster than the company's lawyers were able to file for its removal. Hyundai has issued two apologies for the video, which has been the focus of many news reports.

The reaction to Kmart's marketing campaign was generally positive, while Hyundai's was negative; but both companies received the attention of tens of millions of people worldwide. Do you consider either to be a success or a failure? Why?

When & Where: Storytelling Platforms

In the Hyundai example on the previous page, the company lost control of its marketing video as the audience shared it on the Internet. Control is one of many factors that marketers weigh when they storytell online. However, the risk of losing control of your story when you market online is balanced by unprecedented audience access. At any time of day, someone around the globe might click play! These are just some of the media you will need to consider as you select a platform for your marketing story.

- **Print** - From retail packaging to clothing to magazines, print is physical and therefore tied very closely to the geographical location where it is shared.

- **Broadcast** - Television, cable television, and AM/FM radio are incredible (yet expensive) ways to reach millions of people in their homes.

- **Web** - Through desktops, laptops, and newer TVs, there are many ways to tell your story online, including websites, microsites, blogs, ecommerce portals, etc.

- **Mobile** - As tablets and handheld mobile devices grow more and more common, designing for the "on the go" context is critical.

- **Social** - Some communication platforms, like Facebook, Twitter or LinkedIn, are inherently conversational.

- **Live Events** - Conferences, conventions, and other real-time shows hold value for their immediacy and their media life beyond that actual event.

Game:
Once, Twice, Three Times a Story

 30 Minutes   1+ Player

Each platform has its own storytelling value for making your solution's story novel, entertaining, and personal. Using our Dracula SunShield example, tell that solution story in these three different ways:

One for the Punny:
Written Word Only

Storytell using the written word only - no pictures. You must assume that your audience is going to read your story without the benefit of you being there to direct them. Write between 150 and 350 words. Consider Brand Voice and Tone. And don't forget to use expressive presentation techniques like ALL CAPS, *italicized words*, and **bolded words** to communicate your solution.

Two for the Show:
Picture Show, That Is

Storytell using only images, no words. You can use photographs or drawings that you create yourself or find via a Google image search. Use images with no text on them at all. There's no limit to how many images you can use, but four to five is probably ideal. Arrange them in a sequence or layout that communicates the solution story to the viewer.

Three to Get Ready:
Speak Your Mind! Spoken Word Only

Storytell using spoken word only - no script! Explain your solution to your audience, face to face, just as you did in the Elevator Pitch game (p. 127), but this time, don't rush. Take three to five minutes to storytell in detail and try to excite your audience. Have a solid beginning, middle, and end so that your audience clearly understands your solution and call to action.

Hand off the first and second versions of your story to another person, and then perform your third. How did your audience react to each version? Which was the most effective storytelling medium? How much of the effectiveness was influenced by your solution, and how much was the result of your personal skill set? What type of story would work best on which platform? What might be the benefits of combining these storytelling techniques, or taking the strongest elements of each?

Activity:
Splatter Your Marketing Matrix

 45 Minutes    1 Player

You have so many platforms to choose from that you need to Splatter your storytelling, too! Pick one of your favorite brands, or use one of your own, and write it in the center of the page. Then, write or sketch storytelling ideas under each platform. Sketch in ways that connect the different platforms, too.

Broadcast

A radio commercial of a man and woman talking to explain a translation solution brand

Social

Print

_____

Your Brand Here

Live

Web

Mobile

A crossword puzzle game app for a Dictionary brand

THE STORYTELL CHALLENGE!

Hold a three-day marketing marathon! Over the course of 72 hours, you're going to take a solution through the branding process, and then dream up a dynamite story to introduce it to your audience!

You can work with a solution that you designed with the help of this book, or pick a pre-existing solution that you adore. If you decide to go with a solution that already exists, jettison its established brand and work with the solution itself. So, for example, if you pick Speck mobile device cases, just use "device cases," or if you pick Nike shoes, just focus on "gym shoes."

Are you ready to get started?! Here's an overview of the next three days:

Day 1: Build Your Brand - Build out a brand bible for your solution. Use the activity sheets on the following pages to help you gather and focus your bible content. Then, transfer that copy to a new format: Create a booklet from loose leaf paper, or lay it out on a poster board. Add more details, such as fonts, that you feel fit your brand, or build a custom color palette. Don't forget to develop Voice and Tone (p.122); but rather than illustrating your brand, grab inspirational images from the Internet, or take your own photographs. You could even design your own logo!

Day 2: Mastermind Your Marketing - Decide on the who/what/where/why/when of your solution's story. What is the ideal reaction you want your audience to have after experiencing your story? This is your *call to action* (p.126). Keep that in mind as you brainstorm novel, entertaining, and personal (p.129) ways to tell your story. For this challenge, you may have limitations, like time and budget. Get creative! You can shoot a video on your mobile device and share it via YouTube for maximum exposure at minimal cost.

Day 3: Storytell! - Execute your marketing plan, and share your branded solution story with your audience! If you have been working through this book with a group of people, they will be the final audience for your marketing. Dedicate a full day to storytelling, and of course, collect audience feedback. If you've been designing solo, share you story with a friend via an appropriate platform to gather audience feedback.

CHALLENGE HELP: Brand Building

Consider the unique Brand Promise (p.120) that your solution offers to its audience. Go back to your the Challenge statement you've been evolving throughout your adventures and evolve that into your Brand Promise.

CHALLENGE STATEMENT		
Make this activity...	improved in this way (more, less...)	for these people:

BRAND PROMISE		
This solution	offers this fix or improvement	for these people:

CHALLENGE HELP: Brand Building

Your Universal Truth (p. 121) expresses the human need for your solution, or a desire for the improvement that your brand promises. Remember, every solution has many Universal Truths. Write down a couple here and then pick your favorite! The Universal Truth that you select will influence the kind of story you tell.

SPARK

Considering these problems...	we'll spark solution ideas by asking:

UNIVERSAL TRUTH

Considering these problems...	we'll share these enticing messages:

Dear Dr. Spotlight,
I turn bright red when more than two people look in my direction. How do I storytell without blushing and sweating?

– Mr. Nervous Marketing

Dear Mr. NM,

Oftentimes, the fear of presenting comes from not knowing what to say. Getting a solid handle on your solution story through branding is one of the best ways to know your story inside out and upside down. There is no better fuel for giving a confident presentation than knowing your material.

Not everyone enjoys storytelling in front of a crowd, and that's OK. If stage fright's got you down, that won't stop you from being an awesome marketer. Although there is no substitute for your genuine passion for your story, here are a few tips to keep in mind when you're sharing that brand story:

- Record your speech alone or with just one good friend. Pretend that you are talking to your friend and no one else. She can record you, and you can share it with the world later.
- Look above your audience's heads. Not looking people in the eyes is a good way to keep your mind on task. And they won't even notice where you're looking!
- Have a "pause" plan. If you need to stop and think while delivering a presentation, have a gesture or action at the ready that can buy you time, like taking a sip of water.
- Be the director. Not into being in front of the camera? Maybe you should be behind it. Write a script and have some outgoing pals act it out.

Going It Alone?

If you don't have a group to present to, you always have social media! Myriad social media platforms, including professional ones like Behance, encourage designers such as yourself to share their work and gather feedback.

Want to Make It Real?

If you really believe in your brand, you can always submit it to the ultimate test: an investor! Online crowd-funding platforms like Kickstarter or Quirky will take submissions without robust financial plans (like a financial investment group might want). Be sure to check those sites' submission guidelines before diving in.

Challenges You Can Chew

Salivating for Storytelling?

Learn about the roots of storytelling and be inspired:

The Power of Myth
by Joseph Campbell

Watch expert storytellers spin tales and give tips:
ted.com/topics/storytelling

Silly for Sharing?

Pitch to real investors!

- Kickstarter.com
- Quirky.com

Share your solution, and get expert feedback from pros:

- Behance.net
- Slideshare.net
- LinkedIn.com

The Debrief

Uhm, WOW. You are amazing. You took your solution and gave it a unique personality with branding. Then, you strategically crafted an engaging story for your solution, which all adds up to an active audience responding to your call to action! Congratulations! Now, it's time to do it all over again. Seriously. Storytelling is not a one-way street. Have you ever listened to a story and not reacted to it when the storyteller was done? Storytelling is a form of communication. So, you need to listen to your audience feedback and go back through the design process armed with those insights! Your solution should evolve along with the conversation as you **STORYTELL**.

Holy guacamole! There are no more chapters! Fear not, that does not mean your adventure is complete. It's actually just beginning! Turn the page to learn more about what's in store for you as you choose the next steps in your adventure.

Coming Down from the Mountain

Congratulations on finishing the path! There's a whole lot more to learn, but you now have a taste for it. If you want to keep going, check out some of the Challenges You Can Chew at the end of each chapter. Take your solution – or a new one – through the path again. Or go on new adventures at adventuresxd.com, like these:

Scavenger Hunt

Continue the hunt for photos of good design and bad. Take pictures of things that delight you, such as color patterns you enjoy, or images that evoke an emotion like anger or joy. Post them to a personal blog and describe the meaning behind your choices. Challenge others to post theirs!

Take on Frustration

The next time something frustrates you—a process or product, for example—*design* something about it. Explore Solution Ideas and sketch concepts around them. See if you can create some kind of prototype and test your idea with others. If your solution works well, tell its story to those who may be able to build it.

A Modeled Citizen

Does a particular group of people intrigue you? For example, those in careers that you want to explore? Interview several people from that group and create profiles. What differences and similarities do they have? What characteristics seem to be part of a pattern (and why)?

Five Ways to Resume

Let's say you're about to interview for a job or a college. What will the interviewer want to know? How can you tell the story of your skills and experience? Can you present your resume or portfolio in a way that is easy to understand and compelling? Design the experience of interviewing YOU for five different audiences.

Activity Answers & Resources

Menu from Maître Do, Maître Don't (page 12)

Appetizers

French Fries... $4

Steak Cut, Crinkle Cut or Tater Tot
> with ketchup... 50¢
> with mayo... 50¢

Salad... $5

Tomatos, onions, green peppers and croutons on romaine lettuce with Ranch, Balsamic Vinagrette, Thousand Island or Italian dressing

Entrees

Chicago-Style Hot Dog... $4

Tomatos, mustard, relish, onions on a poppyseed bun
> with tofu dog... Add $2

New York-Style Pizza... $3
> Cheese only
> Pepperoni... Add $1
> Sausage... Add $1

Tandoori Chicken... $10
> with basmati rice

Dragon Roll... $12

Tuna, salmon and shrimp topped with tobiko

Fettucine Alfredo... $10

with chickien... Add $5

Tacos... $8

Steak or chicken with onions, cilantro, sour cream and a side of rice and beans

Southwestern-Style Omelette... $9

Ham, cheddar, onions, green peppers with a side of hash browns

Drinks

Can of soda pop... $1

Sparkling water... $3

Fresh-squeezed orange juice... $2

Thai iced coffee... $2

Hot coffee (with cream and/or sugar)... $1.50

Lasso the Leaders (page 15)

Circle the questions that are badly worded, and explain why.

B. WHY ARE YOU ALWAYS LATE FOR WORK?

F. WHY DON'T YOU FLOSS MORE?

B uses the extreme word "always," which is unlikely true. Both B and F make it sound like you're accusing the people you're interviewing of being unhealthy or irresponsible, which will make them uncomfortable and may affect their answers. For example, people who are feeling defensive may say that they floss more often than they really do, so they don't appear to have unhealthy habits.

C. TELL ME WHY YOU LIKE THIS PAINTING.

D. WHAT MAKES JENNIFER LAWRENCE SUCH A GREAT ACTOR?

If the person has already said before this that she likes the painting, or that she thinks Jennifer Lawrence is a great actor, then these questions are good. If she hasn't, though, you're making an assumption about how she feels when you ask these questions. She may not like the painting at all, and may not agree that Jennifer Lawrence is a great actor - but to be polite she's unlikely to disagree with you when the question assumes she does.

Answers: Find the Fake (page 19)

☑ Fake ☐ Genuine   ☐ Fake ☑ Genuine   ☑ Fake ☐ Genuine   ☑ Fake ☐ Genuine   ☐ Fake ☑ Genuine

Talk Sketchy to Me Words/Phrases (page 57)

(page 57)

- Don't swim here, there are sharks!

- Walk North on the street, take a left at the coffee shop and the hot dog stand is across the street, next to the barber shop.

- The witch has long curly hair and three warts on her nose.

- My dog has 6 legs and long ears. Her name is Rose.

- The racecar jumped off the ramp, went through three rings of fire and landed on the pirate ship.

- I like mushrooms and pepperoni on my pizza.

- If you sing in front of the cyclops, he will go to sleep.

Our Approach: Sketch for a Cook (page 103)

We dropped the soufflé question, relying on the player (or his partner) to know his own level. Here's how we fit the rest:

Name That Brand (page 117)

1. If you get a boo-boo or a scrape, you might put one of these adhesive wound coverings over it: Band-Aid

2. You might tread through this fake green grass on a professional football field: AstroTurf

3. Kids love to "pop" the air-filled plastic pockets on this packaging material, which is often used to protect fragile objects during travel: Bubble Wrap

4. This toy disc glides through the air horizontally. You might play catch with it at the park: Frisbee

5. Regardless of the search engine you are using, this brand name is often used when you are searching a term or phrase on the Internet: Google

6. This popular table-top game is a lot like tennis, but it uses paddles and much smaller, lighter balls: Ping Pong

7. You've probably written yourself a reminder on these little yellow notes, which have an adhesive strip on their back: Post-It Notes

8. You clean your ears with these cotton-tipped swab sticks: Q-Tips

Index